ASPECTS of EXETER

PETER THOMAS
JACQUELINE WARREN

HALSGROVE

First published in Great Britain in 1980 and 1981
This new edition published by Halsgrove in 2006

Research and text and some early photographs are by Jacqueline Warren.
Peter Thomas provided all the photographic work, and the majority of the
photographs are from his Isca Collection.

British Library Cataloguing-in-Publication Data
A CIP record for this title is available from the British Library

ISBN 1 84114 510 6
ISBN 978 1 84114 510 5

HALSGROVE
Halsgrove House
Lower Moor Way
Tiverton, Devon EX16 6SS
Tel: 01884 243242
Fax: 01884 243325
email: sales@halsgrove.com
website: www.halsgrove.com

Printed and bound by CPI Bath

CONTENTS

Acknowledgments

For assistance in the preparation of this publication I should like to thank the following: Exeter City Library (Westcountry Studies Section); The Devon and Exeter Institution, The Customs and Excise, Wheatons, Dingles, Royal Albert Memorial Museum, Martins Caravans, The Cowick Barton, Manpower, The Ashley Countryside Collection and Devon and Cornwall Constabulary.

My sincere thanks are extended to the Late Arthur Everett, Mr. Badcoe (late Headmaster Episcopal School) and Mrs L.B. Steer (Late). A special 'thank you' to Mr R. Cornish, Mr S. Salter, Mr Sampson, Mr S. Mallett, Mr Elliott, Mr M. Voogt and to all of those who have allowed me to use their premises for photographic purposes either on the roof or from obscure windows and who have taken an interest in my work.

I am greatly indebted once again to my brother Clive for his continued interest and practical support.

To my parents my continuing affections for all their help and interest for which I cannot repay.

I cannot thank enough my friend Jan, without whom a considerable amount of this material may not have been seen. In particular for the hours spent sorting 40,000 negatives. I am greatly indebted to him.

Lastly to Charles who assisted me and took me to many locations around Exeter, and my thanks for the hours spent sorting photographs and above all for his support when times were difficult.

P. THOMAS, 1980

I am grateful to the East Devon Library Services, and particularly to the staff of the Westcountry Studies Room, for helping me find the documents and publications which I needed in the preparation of this work. I also thank Mr C.G. Bastone for reading my manuscript and making useful suggestions for its improvement.

J. WARREN

Jacqueline and Bob Warren, after their marriage in Paris, settled in Exeter, where their three children – born in the 1940s – were educated, until they left for universities and college of music.

Mrs Warren became specifically interested in the buildings and history of the city in the 1950s, but this interest was combined with her general interest in architecture and townscape which was greatly increased in the course of numerous visits to Italian cities and towns to study their buildings.

Jacqueline Warren has contributed travel and other articles to *The Times*, *The Guardian*, *The Sunday Times*, to magazines, to professional journals such as *Building Design* and *Road Tar*, and to the local and regional newspapers on local history and buildings. She also has given a series of lectures on Exeter to the Workers' Educational Association (WEA).

In recognition of her specialised knowledge, Mrs Warren was appointed Curator of St Nicholas Priory by Exeter City Council when the post became vacant in 1959. She left this employment in 1973 when the post of Curator was suppressed, the Council having decided to turn this historic monument into a little museum.

Until her death in 1991 Jacqueline continued to research and write articles for national and regional publications and she kept an ever-vigilant eye on Exeter's townscape and architecture, the city she so loved.

French-born, Jacqueline Warren was educated in Paris, after which she went abroad to spend several months in England and in Spain to study the languages of these countries.

It was in the course of one of her English visits that she met her future husband, Bob, who was studying engineering in London. His father and uncle were the Warren Brothers of the then well-known firm established in Exeter for some 100 years, but which ceased to exist when its premises were destroyed in the bombing of 1942. Charles Warren had been Mayor of Exeter in 1930/31.

Educated at Episcopal Secondary Modern School at Mount Dinham, Exeter, he started work at the age of 15 in the building trade with a building company who specialised in stone restoration. He used photography to record the restoration of ancient churches and general building sites.

After five years he joined a well-known photographic retail outlet in Princesshay, Exeter, where he worked for 14 years.

During this period his interest in photography turned towards its history and the collecting of photographic antiques. In 1974, by accident, he acquired the entire negative stock of the city's last true photographic studio – the Henry Wykes Studio in Northernhay Place. This consisted of approximately 42,000 images of Exeter. To protect this unique resource he established the Isca Historical Photographic Collection. It has been greatly enlarged over the years.

The Collection started a lifetime fascination with images of Exeter and led to him to becoming a local author, publishing his first book *Old Exeter*, in 1977. It was an instant success. At this time only one other local history book was available.

Focusing his attention and concerns towards the changing face of his city he persuaded the well-known local freelance writer Jacqueline Warren to join him in a major work designed to attract public

Exonian, Peter Thomas, was born in 1948 at historic Poltimore House near Exeter and has lived and worked in Exeter all his life. Today he is the longest established author of local history books on the City of Exeter and a specialist on Exeter's photographic history.

From an early age he was interested in photography, this being due to the encouragement of his godmother, Doris Aldridge, a professional singer and lecturer. This fascination with photography has continued throughout his life.

attention towards the plight of the city. It was to be the result of three years' work and called *Aspects of Exeter*. It was launched in 1981. A controversial publication at the time, again it was an instant sell out and today is acknowledged as an important educational and historical resource on a specific period in the city's history.

Aspects of Exeter was accepted by HRH Prince Charles and exhibited in St James Palace in 1981.

Such was the public interest that a continuing number of books have been produced over a period of 30 years, all promoting the city through its photographic history, of which Peter is now a specialist. He has lectured extensively over the years, creating some of the largest audiovisual presentations the city has ever seen, using local theatres with audiences of up to 500 people. As a lecturer he has covered numerous subjects from Exeter to Mexico, having a particular interest in conservation and natural history.

As a freelance photographer he has undertaken numerous types of work with an extensive archive created for the book *Images of Devon*, covering the whole county in numerous aspects. This was quickly followed by a further project on the whole of Dorset for the book *Dorset Moods*. As a specialist in images, work has followed creating videos and dvds including 'Old Exeter', 'The Classic Old Exeter' and 'The Exeter Blitz'.

In 1985 Peter joined Exeter City Council, becoming Exeter's first Tourism Promotion Officer in 1987. He instigated 'The famous Exeter Red Coat Guides' and Exeter Guided Tours, a project that brought 450,000 people to visit the city. In 1986 he staged the largest historical exhibition seen in the city, 'The Great Exeter Exhibition', attracting thousands of people. During a 14-year period much of the city's hidden history was opened up by him including Exeter's strangest attraction, 'The Exeter Catacomb'. Of major appeal was the creation of the Exeter Historical Pageant, with hundreds of Exeter citizens taking part, this being extended into a major heritage weekend with the development of Exeter's first Medieval Fayre in 1998.

The exhibition 'The bombing of Exeter', held in Rougemont House, Exeter in 1992, was the largest exhibition ever shown on the Second World War in Exeter and visited by hundreds of people.

As a local personality, author and local historian, Peter has taken part in TV documentaries, radio interviews and events.

Today he actively continues his work on the City together with freelance photographic work and running a photo library. His work has been responsible for laying important foundation stones for promoting interest in the county's local history.

The ISCA Collection

Established in 1974 by Peter Thomas, The Isca Historical Photographic Collection was set up to protect a unique photographic archive relating to the work of Exeter photographer Henry Wykes. The Wykes Studio, started at the turn of the century at Exe Bridge, was finally located at Northernhay Place. On its closure in 1974 the studio negative stock was acquired in order to retain it for posterity. The commercial work consisted of approximately 42,000 half-plate negatives and is a unique historical resource.

Over a period of 30 years the Collection has been greatly expanded to contain more photographic material now covering the city from 1860 to the present day. Prints, albums, lantern slides, negatives, postcards, etchings, engravings, paintings, transparencies etc. have all been added. It is the largest private archive relating to the history of Exeter and contains rare images. The Isca Collection was used for the first photo history book of Exeter *Old Exeter* in 1977. Over the years a number of books have been produced together with the first historic Exeter videos and DVDs, including *Old Exeter* and *The Exeter Blitz*. Recently a range of archive greetings cards have been produced to promote the Collection.

The Isca Collection has been extensively used for lecturing purposes giving hundreds of people the opportunity to see Exeter as it was over a period of 150 years. Archive images have been used for major exhibitions, promotional features and used for television documentaries, theatrical productions and collaborative projects. The City Council's guided tour service also benefited from the collection as archive images from the Collection formed part of the training program for the famous Red Coat Guides, Exeter's voluntary tourist guides, giving them a unique insight into the historic city.

The Isca Historical Photographic Collection has undertaken some the largest audio visual projects ever seen in Exeter for audiences of up to 500 people. In particular the program 'The bombing of Exeter in Sight and Sound' captured the public's attention. It presented cinema screen size images to the public together with appropriate wartime sound effects.

The Collection is registered with The Royal Photographic Society in the Historical Collection Directory. It has been recognised by the National Monuments Record Centre of English Heritage as being of Local, Regional and National interest. The Imperial War Museum has supported the Collection.

Introduction to the First Edition

The purpose of this book is mostly to give some idea of what Exeter might have been still, if it had not suffered the air raids of 1942, and if a misguided conception of improvement, before and after the war, had not resulted in the undiscerning demolition of so many of its buildings.

So this book is about some of the losses Exeter has sustained; about some of the replacements, which in many cases have turned out to be unsuitable for their environment; and also about what has been spared, and which is still with us.

If in this latter group our chosen examples do not include the Cathedral, its Close and the Guildhall, it is partly because much is already available in print about them, but also because they are so placed that no one living in Exeter or visiting the city could be unaware of their existence.

Whenever possible, and if of any interest, the buildings mentioned and shown in these pages have served to recall some of the people who were connected with them in the near or distant past.

We feel that our book, showing what has been done to Exeter, may also, as an example, suggest why other cities and towns in Britain have lost much of their individuality and character.

J.W.

Introduction to the New Edition

The introduction to the first edition, written by Jacqueline, clearly states what our aspirations and ideas were. Our collaboration, and resulting long-term friendship, was born out of concern for what was happening in Exeter at the time. But now, 25 years later, have attitudes changed? It will be up to the reader to decide.

During the 1980s and 1990s Exeter was undergoing considerable changes and during this period there appeared to be a more enlightened attitude towards the city's heritage. But let's look at some aspects that have occurred since this book was first published ?

In 1982 the medieval statue of St Peter, located at the corner of North Street and High Street, was taken down for restoration but it was never replaced due to its fragility. A copy could have been made but the alcove remains empty. In 1983 the City Council viewed the Catacombs as a possible tourist attraction but this never transpired, and St Anne's Almshouses in Blackboy Road were to be saved from dereliction. In 1985 a major archaeological dig was underway in Exe Street and Exeter Guided Tours was instigated by The City Council and Manpower Services Commission. In the same year the original Elizabethan Dock at the Quay was discovered and there were high hopes to create a tourist attraction of the Roman Baths in Cathedral Yard.

In 1986 a new Heritage Centre was recommended for the Quay by transforming the original transit shed, and a restoration project proposed for Cricklepit Mill. In 1987 Rougemont House was threatened with collapse due to poor building fabric and it was suggested to give the West Quarter a face lift. The Quay was also earmarked as being the answer to 'a tourism boom' following the creation of the Canal & Quay Trust in 1981, and an archaeological dig started at Magdalen Street near South Gate.

In 1988 there were plans for housing development at Trew's Weir Mills. In 1989 a new style of building was designated for Castle Street to improve the vista.

In 1990 there were new plans for shopping and employment and tourism in Exeter and the Catacombs were finally opened to the public due to the popularity of Exeter Guided Tours. In 1991 Haven Banks were finally cleared of most of its industrial buildings, the site being developed for housing.

In 1995 a substantial site at Smythen Street (originally Evans & Gadd) was sold for redevelopment and in October a campaign was started to save 21 The Mint, once part of St Nicholas Priory, and new Roman remains were uncovered at Broadgate.

In 1996 the redevelopment of Cricklepit Mill hung in the balance and the pressure was on to promote Exeter Quay. The old Evans & Gadd Art Deco building failed to be saved and was later demolished. Exeter Maritime Museum was to close and the city lost a major attraction. In 1997 The Civic Society promoted a scheme to turn the empty Custom House into a Smuggling Museum but the plan was rejected.

In 1999 there were proposals to give the Guildhall Shopping Centre a facelift and strong objections came from English Heritage with regard to the rebuilding of the city centre. Plans were published to change the Eye Infirmary in Magdalen Street into a hotel, now called The Hotel Barcelona, and the project saved an important building. In October it was announced that the city centre was to be redeveloped.

In 2000 Exeter Museum was in the news with fears about its future and there were more redevelopment proposals for the Basin. The City Council gave more money to preserve the staircase and ceilings of the Custom House. The new scheme for Princesshay received public objections and an opposition group formed. In April plans to redevelop the bus station site were proposed and the conversion of Cricklepit Mill started. In June, Queen Street was repaved at a cost of £250,000.

In very recent times the upper High Street was stated as being one of the most uninspiring in the country, being paved with Chinese granite, and given the title 'The Worst Clone Street in the Country'.

These are only a few aspects of developments missed or undertaken over the last 25 years. At the present time there is a massive building site incorporating Paris Street, Princesshay Post Office Street and Bedford Street. Earlier buildings were demolished.

Today all available space is being redeveloped and as the populations grows so does the congestion. It appears that Exeter is marking the end of an era with a fundamental change to the look of the city. It is hoped that this book will, again, raise interest in the preservation, enhancement and protection of the Exeter's historic fabric and its character for the future generations.

Peter Thomas

About this Book

FROM THE FIRST EDITION

Exeter, capital of Devon, which has a history going back nearly 2,000 years, celebrated in 1980 the 1900th anniversary of its foundation as a self-governing civil community.

I wonder what the average impression is of the visitor to Exeter? Certainly the Cathedral and its Close will impress him, together with the Guildhall, but what about the residents? Are they happy with their city? As an Exonian, the view of residents has always interested me and it was because of my own interests and photographic pursuits that I had published *Old Exeter*, a book of photos of pre-war Exeter aimed at the man in the street. This publication is still in demand and has, it seems, stimulated an interest in the lost aspects of our city. Here then, is another book, and one of a very different nature. I had long felt that from my collection of pre-war material something very significant could appear, and now, in collaboration with Jacqueline Warren, I feel this has been achieved.

For many years conflicts have arisen in Exeter with regard to its historic buildings and its rebuilding after sustaining war damage. However, there has been no publication to my knowledge that has dealt with the subject in any depth. Much overlooked, I feel, has been the destruction of the City's character. It can be said that this book is about environmental change. However, it goes further than that, since parts relating to the city's general and social history, and to its architecture and townscape, can also be found in it. It has been both my intention and Jacqueline Warren's, that we present a highly illustrated book combined with an authoritative and detailed text. I feel we have achieved this, but obviously it will be up to the reader to judge.

For today's generation, I think it is essential that as much material as possible should be available to encourage an interest in their local environment and in protecting their heritage. A point, I feel, which is not usually put over strongly enough. It is pointless to despair after a unique building or townscape has been demolished. Awareness is all important, and then, perhaps, further mistakes can be avoided. Mistakes have been made in Exeter, but although the bad ones are unpleasant to live with, they can also serve as examples not to follow.

Because of the scope of this particular project, I decided it was essential to seek help on the text. My enquiries led me to Jacqueline Warren. She has written articles about Exeter in a number of newspapers, journals, etc., for over 20 years, and without doubt her knowledge is extremely wide with regard to the city's history.

Most of the pictures in this book are unique. I think that anyone would agree that several of the comparisons between what was on a certain site once, and what is there now, are quite startling. Personally, because Exeter is continually changing, I have found the time aspect in the compiling of this work, quite fascinating. Indeed, to be able to record visually, certain features of this city, the time factor was crucial. Exeter today continues to expand, and its history will progress into the future. I hope however, that after reading this book and looking at the illustrations, our readers will reflect a little more on the past and on what may happen in the future.

P.T.

CHAPTER 1

North Street

The picturesque east side of North Street was destroyed in the early 1970s and replaced by grim and forbidding prison-like walls raised to contain the premises of supermarkets and chain-stores which are part of the new Guildhall Shopping Centre, an area known once, in avid anticipation, as The Golden Heart.

The demolished side of North Street comprised several scheduled buildings of architectural or historic interest, but it was the delightful mixture of various styles, on a small scale, which formed the charm of the townscape between Waterbeer Street and Paul Street.

At the Paul Street end, there was a fine fifteenth-century timber roof in at least one of the buildings. This was part of a group of ancient timber-framed houses, and 'The Elephant' actually retained part of its old inn yard at the back, as well as an attractive stone wall projecting forward at first and second floor levels.

The Church of St Kerrian was demolished in 1878, but its remains: the brick porch, bell turret, clock, and the base of the church walls left in position just above the road level, all added to the visual pleasure experienced when glancing at this side of the street.

Chudley's premises, No. 44, was a single building of much charm. It was early-nineteenth century; in perfect condition; and one of the only two examples in Exeter of a house with taper-framed windows. These also had attractive iron balconies.

But the most unforgiveable was the demolition of

Nos. 19 and 20 North Street. Demolished 1890.

'The Last Judgement' wall monument removed from St. Kerrian's Church, North Street.

Old North Street (c.1880). Now Cornish's and Hepworth's premises left and right.

North Street in 1980 at the corners with Paul Street and Bartholomew Street East.

Wasteland and rear of North Street houses, 1979. (See text).

The passageway to the back of No. 18 North Street, 1980. Probably early-seventeenth century.

The rear of No. 18 North Street in dilapidated condition today and worthy of restoration. (Early-seventeenth century.)

No. 38 (Mansfield's antique shop). It had been thought, mistakenly, to be a fake, because of the rebuilding in the last century of its seventeenth-century façade, but this house was not even reprieved when the city's own archaeologists found that not only was part of the building really 300 years old, but also that some of its interesting features dated from as early as the fifteenth century.

Most of the houses on the western side of North Street look as if they had been built in the nineteenth century – the time when in that street one could buy for 3d. at the British Workmen's Restaurant, slices of beef and gravy to take away – but the nineteenth century fronts to some of these houses are deceptive. Several of them are much older, as we can see if we look at them from what must have been their gardens once, and which is now part of a wasteland beside a multi-storey car park.

The back of No. 18 North Street, gabled, with an oriel window supported by brackets, shows that the building probably dates from the early-seventeenth century. This would also be the date of its interesting passageway to North Street which has a doorway with moulded jambs; an entirely pegged wooden screen with panels between rails and stiles; a massive beam across its ceiling; and the original flagstones on the floor.

The backs of Nos 16 and 17 are also gabled and evidently belong to the same period as No. 18. Parts of colourful walls of Heavitree and other local stone, and some cobbles, remain at the back of Nos 19/20. These were a pair of houses whose handsome, carved-oak façade was an attractive feature in North Street until, in 1890, it was 'modernised'. One of the bay windows of No. 19, and some of the oak work of this fine façade, were incorporated into the altered front of No. 229 High Street (once Lyons's premises) in the early 1930s.

Considering how few of the small, domestic buildings belonging to Exeter's past have survived, it is a pity that those which still remain should become the victims of years of neglect so that their eventual crumbling condition can be used as an excuse for their demolition.

CHAPTER 2

No. 38 North Street
(Mansfield's Antique Galleries)

In recent years, we had two houses in Exeter whose facades were typical of the second half of the seventeenth century. Now we have one, No. 227 High Street, Austin Reed's premises. The other was demolished in 1972. It was No. 38 North Street, which had been Mansfield's Antique Galleries, but which was bought by the city council in 1966 and allowed to decay, since the intention was to demolish the whole east side of North Street, in order to erect the forbidding structure which we can now see there.

In spite of some reconstruction at the end of the last century to the Mansfield building (part of the house was removed for road widening) its carefully rebuilt front was full of the interesting characteristics of the seventeenth-century town house: slate-hung gables, bracketed bay windows, a gallery with balustrade in front of three round-headed windows,

the projecting one being surmounted by a pediment.

This house originally comprised a three-bay open hall in its centre, with three-storey blocks at each end. As a merchant's house it would have had a shop at the front. The main walls were built of the local Heavitree stone (a coarse, red sandstone incorporating angular fragments of other stones) and partitions were timber framed. The arch-braced roof survived.

After the city council had resolved to demolish this building, having decided that it was an architectural fake, the archaeologists moved in and discovered that it was not, in spite of the 1889 alterations. There was a beautiful seventeenth-century plaster ceiling in the first-floor front room, but by removing lath and plaster covering, such features as fifteenth-century open fireplaces and mullioned windows were revealed.

There was also a kitchen block at the back of the house, with a large stone stack to the hearth and a bread oven.

In the early 1870s, George and Charles Finch, of the Eagle Brewery, carried on business at No. 144 Fore Street, but by 1878, they had also acquired the

Mansfields exterior (c.1900) showing rebuilt seventeenth-century façade after road widening.

Gallery in Inner Court.   (J.W.)

Early-seventeenth-century interior as revealed during demolition in 1972.

(J.W.)

The fifteenth-century fireplace exposed during demolition.
(J.W.)

premises of No. 38 North Street. The Eagle Brewery was still at the North Street address in the early 1890s, but it was later succeeded by the Burton Brewery. As for Frank George Mansfield, the cabinet-maker, he had been established for some time at No. 33 North Street and it was not until early in this century – probably in 1902 – that he moved to No. 38. The same family carried on business at that address for nearly 70 years. The demolition of such a building was a great loss to Exeter.

Sources
Personal observation at the time the building was being stripped, and the reports of archaeologists in charge of the site.
Nineteenth and twentieth-century Besley's Directories.

CHAPTER 3

Exe Street, Lower North Street and Northernhay Street

If we consider what elements make a landscape, a village, or a town attractive, we shall nearly always find that one of the most important is the unevenness of the ground. The rising hill, the steep lane, the sloping garden, tiers of terraces, have in themselves a charm that level sites rarely attain whatever may be their other attributes.

The south-eastern side of Exe Street is almost completely filled by 'The Lower Cemetery', which spreads upward to the fortress-like catacombs and Bartholomew Yard. On the other side of this street stood a row of cottages whose little back yards were tight against the cliff that rises to Mount Dinham.

Some of these cottages formed Culver Place, which recalled that the high Wear Cliff site above, before it became Mount Dinham, was named Culver Park (there, until the early-nineteenth century, was also a rackfield). Tremletts Cottages, a little further on towards Lower North Street, were a good example of how various levels and a contrast between the horizontal and the vertical can give character to a place and make it visually interesting. Nine steps

gave access to a narrow way formed by the side walls of houses fronting Exe Street. The alleyway widened and reached the façade of a low cottage built against the cliff, behind which soared the spire of St Michael's Church.

The site of all these cottages has become a car park, and above this, where once until a few years ago, gardens below Mount Dinham sloped down attractively, now stands an imitation Georgian terrace which, from Bartholomew Street East, is a confusing, unfortunate sight, mingling as it does, visually, with the houses of Mount Dinham.

The site above the north-western side of Exe Street was purchased by John Dinham in 1860, and there he had 24 cottages erected (more were added later) to provide rent-free homes for people in 'reduced circumstances', but who were not destitute, and who, preferably, were over 60 years of age.

Exe Lane, as this street was still called in 1835, was once part of a favourite walk for Exonians, along the Long Brook, which then flowed unfettered towards the river. The brook is now piped. At the Bonhay end of Exe Lane was the water-engine which supplied the city with water, and this is recalled in an inscription above the doorway of the corner shop which is by the leat bridge. This group of small Victorian houses was erected in 1887 and named Engine Bridge Buildings. Twelve houses of that period remain in this part of Exe Street, including the Papermakers' Arms, but two-thirds of them are derelict and have been so for sometime.

On the brook side of the lane, fields forming the south-eastern slope of the valley rose towards the city wall until 1837, when the catacombs were built and the fields became The Lower Cemetery (used as such until 1949, now a public garden). On the right of it, facing the garden, we can see the Barbican Steps picturesquely climbing to the green of Bartholomew Yard.

At the other end of The Lower Cemetery, in Exe Street, were Napier Terrace and, a little further on, Cemetery Place. The houses of the latter were older than the early Victorian ones of the former, but both rose to the top of the valley in a picturesque series of steps. Cemetery Place was allowed to decay and to vanish, but Napier Terrace is looking delightful thanks to the brightness of all its houses whose occupants lovingly maintain. Unfortunately, following the steps, a wall has been built thoughtlessly to such a height that it is no longer possible for the inhabitants of the Napier Terrace houses to enjoy the view

Renovated cottages in Northernhay Street.

View of the Iron Bridge spanning the Longbrook Valley showing (right) construction of new houses in Lower North Street and Northernhay Street.

View of the Iron Bridge from Lower North Street.

This photograph shows the original level of Lower North Street before 1834.

The Iron Bridge over the Longbrook Valley taken from the City Wall.

of the adjoining public garden from their ground-floor front rooms.

It is as we approach it from Exe Street that the graceful shape of the Iron Bridge can be best appreciated. We can then see it sideways and admire the excellence of proportion which has succeeded in giving elegance to this work whose first quality had to be strength. It might never have spanned the Longbrook Valley, however, if Queen Street had been planned earlier, for all the traffic to and from North Devon could have taken that convenient new route.

A resident of Lower North Street complained a few years ago that heavy lorries were using it, although it is only 7ft 7in. wide at its narrowest point, and remarked that the street was made for horses and carriages, not lorries. True, but an observer in

the last century wrote of the traffic there in the 1820s, 'I have seen from 12 to 20 pair-horse carts in succession laden with lime and coming from the St Leonard and Countess Wear kilns,' and we might wonder whether iron-rimmed wheels and horses' shoes on cobbles were not as tiresome as lorries in low gear.

But this was before the Iron Bridge was erected, when vehicles from North Devon came over St David's Hill and down the descent to the Plume and Feathers, passing the Barnstaple Inn, and then went up North Street. The traffic up and down was almost continuous and it surprises that heavily laden carts could negotiate such gradients. Although the North Gate was demolished in 1769 (a plaque shows where it was opposite the Crown and Sceptre Hotel), the road which went through it remained steep and the dip in Lower North Street was deeper than it is today, its level being that of Exe Street.

Eventually, something had to be done about the level of the ground between St David's Hill and North Street, and in 1834 Russell & Brown of Worcester built the Iron Bridge. Its massive units were brought by road and water as there was no railway here. The then residents of the street fought fiercely against the project, and there was disagreement among the authorities regarding the position of the bridge. One side wanted it to be built in a direct line with the upper part of North Street, and the decision to have it slightly to the west of this position (where it is) was reached by a majority of one.

Exe Street from the Lower Cemetery showing below the spire of St Michael's. A pseudo Georgian terrace.

A group of seven eighteenth-century houses remains in Lower North Street, but there is an unfortunate gap where the Bridge Inn was (it was burned down some years ago). It is from this part of the street that we can best see the attractive Iron Bridge. In the dip nearby was once St Anne's Brewery, and here, underground, the piped Longbrook is on its way to the river. Further on, where Lower North Street rises towards St David's Hill, we can see an interesting seventeeth-century building which must once have been a farmhouse. It has a typical parvis (a jutting, pillar-supported porch with a small room above it). This building – unique of its kind in Exeter – restored and with some modernisation of its interior, could be a marvellous house to live in.

If we walk in Lower North Street towards Paul Street and turn left before reaching it, we enter Northernhay Street. It follows the outside of the city wall, which can be seen on and off along the length of this street on its south side.

At the corner of Paul Street, Lower North Street and Northernhay Street, houses are being built. One can see at the moment (August 1978) that the foundations of the buildings being demolished were the city wall itself.*

The best view of the outer face of the wall is further up the street, from what used to be a stone-mason's yard, a site now occupied by the Electricity Board. On this side of the street, one of the eighteenth-century houses has been renovated. Continuing up the hill, we come to Maddocks Row, pierced in the city wall in 1772 to give access to Paul Street. Here is an interesting early-eighteenth-century house whose entrance is in Northernhay Street and which had, not so long ago, a pretty garden, now neglected, partly enclosed by the city wall. Next to this house but on the inner side of the city wall, stood in the last century a house whose beautiful garden, in which was a pond, extended along the city wall and covered part of the present open car park of Paul Street.

When the South Gate prison was demolished in 1819, the prisoners were transferred to the new city jail which stood until 1863 on the site of the Rougemont Hotel, on the north side of Northernhay Street. This side of the street has some very attractive, mostly early-eighteenth-century houses, as we can see if we walk back towards Lower North Street. Nos. 14 to 18 are cottages, mostly renovated, and No. 16 is being very well restored by its owner himself.

Napier Terrace (off Exe Street) rising to the City Wall in Bartholomew Street.

Tremletts Cottages, Exe Street, a car park in 1980. (J.W.)

Padrae Cottages, under one hipped roof, were built as three cottages. Further down, Northernhay Square, formed by eight small early-Victorian houses and some older ones, is a well-kept, delightful little enclosure.

It is a pity that some of the houses with truncated gables and bracketed porches between Northernhay Square and Lower North Street are so neglected. Renovated as three of them have been, and with the right colour scheme, they could form a handsome group.

Northernhay Street, until the early part of the nineteenth century, was a lane called Northernhay Row. It is pleasing that it has so far retained something valuable from the past in its gradient, width, attractive houses, and scale. But the huge brick wall and double doors erected by the Electricity Board, which would adorn any industrial estate, are out of character and the wrong scale in this picturesque little street. This is a pity, because whatever is done to restore, renovate and maintain what is original in this street to improve it, the conspicuous new feature will be there to mar the total effect

Sources

History of the City of Exeter (A. Jenkins, 1806)
Documents relating to John Dinham (City Archives, Record Office)
Reminiscences of Exeter Fifty Years Since (James Cossins 1878)
Maps of Exeter 1587–1860
Documents in City Archives relating to the Iron Bridge

*The new buildings now form an attractive group whose two-size gables are pleasingly seen from North Street and whose sash windows are in keeping with those of the eighteenth-century buildings in the area. The bricks used in these houses have an attractively rough texture, and access to the courtyard is interestingly through a wide, keystoned archway

Aerial view of Exeter Quay. The Basin and Shilhay (c.1950).

CHAPTER 4

The Quay

To an observant person looking at the façade of Exeter's handsome Custom House, the arches surrounding the entrance door and the ground-floor windows may seem a strange feature. But these belonged to the original arrangement, which was an open arcade so that goods which had just been unloaded at the Quay could easily be brought to shelter. In the eighteenth century, these arches were filled in because by then more enclosed space was needed in the carrying out of various duties within the building.

The Custom House – whose eastward extension dates from the eighteenth century – has often been said to be the first brick building to be erected in Exeter. It was completed externally in 1681, but some work was still going on in 1685. Although Tudor House in Tudor Street, which dates from earlier in the seventeenth century, is partly built of brick, it is true that until the end of that century most Exeter houses were built of stone or cob.

The Custom House's hipped roof, small pediment, bracketed eaves, white corner stones, wide frames round the windows which are flush with the walls, are all typical features of the last quarter of the seventeenth century, which persisted throughout the first quarter of the eighteenth. This Queen Anne style of architecture actually involved five reigns. The Royal Arms on the pediment date from 1820.

Inside, three flights of the massive staircase, and a gallery, form a quadrangle. The handrail over the stout balusters is almost as broad as the newel cap, and the pendants end in large carved flowers. But the treasure of the place is the Long Room upstairs.

Its extravagant Baroque plaster ceiling includes curving oak branches with leaves and acorns, pigs' faces, snakes, flowers, and fruits which are built over sticks and scrim and hang lusciously. This is the work of the famous North Devon plasterer John Abbot of Frithelstock (1639–1727), who was paid £35 for it; the architect, Richard Allen, received a fee of £3.4s.6d. for his design of the building. The Royal Arms, another interesting feature in the Long Room, date from 1707.

There is also at the Custom House a fascinating collection of spits. They are long sharp steel instruments used by Customs Officers to check that top layers of certain cargoes do not conceal the illicit, hidden underneath. Two sharp hooks at the end of one spit's long blade would be used to bring up to the surface small specimens for investigation. The expression 'not to trust further than one can spit' derives from the function of this instrument whose effectiveness is limited to its length.

Some records of the Board of Customs and Excise give valuable information about the Port of Exeter, such as the destination of the ships, the kind of

Exeter Quay showing Warehouses, Cellars and Colleton Crescent (c.1900).

From a painting by Haslehurst.

cargoes they carried, and details about the duties (and sometimes misdemeanour) of the men connected with the port's activity.

The River Exe had been navigable as far as Exeter until Isabella Countess of Devon built a weir, which was irretrievably consolidated by her successor the Earl of Devon, Hugh Courtenay, some 25 years later, that is in 1311. It took almost 300 years of litigation, and the decline in power of the Courtenays, before the weir at Countess Wear could be demolished. But although this was done, the river was by then too silted up for navigation, and so the City Chamber engaged the engineer John Trew to make it navigable from Exmouth to the city. He decided on building a canal which would extend from Countess Wear to a sluice where ships could re-enter the river just before reaching the Quay. The Basin was not built until 1830.

The new waterway was opened in 1566, and a new quay and Water Gate (in the city wall, to give easy access to the city) had also been built. However, only 16 ton vessels could reach the city, the larger ones still had to be unloaded at Topsham or transferred to lighters. But in the last quarter of the seventeenth century, the canal was extended towards Topsham as well as made deeper so that ships of 100 tons could reach Exeter.

The Elizabethan quay was levelled, lengthened, and reinforced with a strong wall, alongside which

The Custom House completed externally in 1681 with eighteenth-century extension.

The Longroom showing plaster ceiling by John Abbot of Frithelstock.

Plaster ceiling in another room of the Custom House.

Left: *The plaster ceiling above the main staircase.*

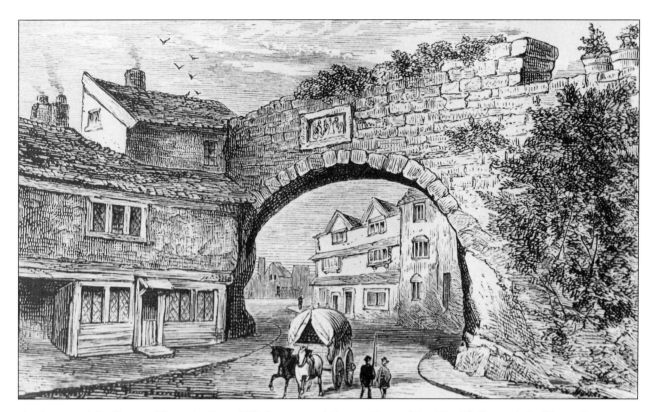

At the rear of the Custom House in Quay Hill, between existing sections of the City Wall, stood the Water Gate.

A ship unloading in the basin in the nineteenth century.

Shipping moored in the basin, c.1890.

ships could lie conveniently to discharge or load their cargoes. No doubt the importance of the woollen trade at the time prompted these improvements. It was soon after they were carried out that the decision to build the Custom House was taken by the City Chamber. It cost the city, to which it still belongs, £3,000.

The charming little red-brick building with a

Dutch gable, separated from the Custom House by the narrow road of Quay Hill, was the Wharfinger's Office. It was built in 1778 when Exeter was still a great port.

The two warehouses on the Quay, built in 1835, are larger than any other building nearby, luckily they are very handsome. Their dark-red volcanic Pocombe stone shot with white veins of quartz, their bright-red brick, and pale-grey limestone, combine a successful colour scheme with an attractive texture, and even the loading platforms contribute to the pleasing effect of these buildings.

The vaulted cellars, a little further on, are another interesting feature of the Quay. Dug out of the red

Exeter Docks, c.1900.

sandstone cliff below Colleton Crescent to a length of 60 feet, the 12 of them were excavated between 1880 and 1906. The first ones were used by local soap and candle manufacturers. These brick-lined, man-made caves are now mostly used as workshops.

It is because these interesting features from the seventeenth, eighteenth and nineteenth centuries are still there that this area remains so fascinating. Even the bollard in front of the warehouses recalls the city's history. Until recently there were four. They were parts of guns supposed to have been used at the Battle of Waterloo, and which had been held in Exeter by the Port Authorities since 1824, when they were on their way to the Wellington Monument.

But another theory is that in 1817, the Prince Regent having promised cannons from the Battle of Waterloo for the Wellington Monument, 16 arrived in Exeter, one being made of brass, the others of iron. However, none was a relic from the famous battle: they had been made in Scotland for Russia! The reason why they stayed in Exeter then, would appear to be that their origin not being what had been expected, they were not accepted by the Wellington Memorial Committee. So, in 1824, the brass cannon was sold by Exeter City Council to pay for dock charges, and four of the iron ones remained on the Quay to become bollards.

Then, in 1893, the 11 others were literally unearthed (they had been buried); four going, after all, to the Wellington Monument; and seven being placed in Bull Meadow (they were melted down during the last war). Two of the bollards were removed from the Quay in 1977 as they obstructed a

The Quay with the Fish Market, c.1930. Most of the buildings at the back of the market no longer exist.

new sewer. One of these was sent to the Wellington Monument; another is still on the Quay; and a third has a bright future: an enthusiastic engineer has offered to provide a new gun carriage for it. It would be made from authentic working drawings of carriages used for guns similar to those which became these bollards. So, we might one day see this gun carriage with the canon mounted on the Quay.

The splendid Maritime Museum is one of the attractions of this area.

Sources
City records (Record Office) Records of the Board of Customs & Excise (Custom House) *Express & Echo* reports: 15 and 19 December 1978.

West Street at the junction with Stepcote Hill before the restoration of the fifteenth-century houses.

The Old West Gate, demolished 1815, viewed from outside the City Wall.

✦ CHAPTER 5 ✦

The West Quarter

The West Quarter, loosely defined as being within the lines formed by South Street, Fore Street, West Street and Coombe Street, was in the days of the woollen trade a wealthy residential part of the city. The summer-house of its fabulous Mermaid Inn was a place where merchants often met and could watch their ships in the harbour below. This summer-house was described then as overlooking 'the gardens of the gentry and rich merchants residing in Preston Street.' Something difficult for us to imagine today.

By the nineteenth century, most of the district had become overcrowded, neglected, and part of it was a slum. Now, after the bombing during the war, and the clearing of some of the houses before and after it, little is left of the original townscape of the West Quarter save for that part of it formed by West Street, Stepcote Hill, the church of St Mary Steps and the fifteenth-century houses beside and opposite the church.

But the early-fifteenth-century house opposite the church was not there originally, it came from Frog Street, some 70 yards below its present position. A few years before, a house of the same size, design and age which stood on the site, had been demolished, so this made it possible for the Frog Street house to be moved to it!

It was moved because Frog Street, which had retained its medieval shape and picturesque appearance, was about to be bulldozed into a wide thoroughfare convenient to motorcars. So the pre-Tudor house, firmly corseted within its wooden stays, was lifted bodily on hydraulic jacks, winched out of its Frog Street site, given temporary wheels, and hauled up the street on rails at a pace of a few inches an hour, on 12 December 1961. It was later well restored, but now (January 1978) shows signs of neglect. Its timber frame and the cusped wooden tracery of its windows show that this is the oldest dwelling-house that Exeter possesses. But since its move it has been used

The view from Stepcote Hill until the 1960s, showing the junction of Edmund Street with Ewings Lane.

The view in 1979.

Houses in Stepcote Hill, West Street, before restoration in the 1930s.

as business premises. The two timber-framed houses beside the church were threatened with demolition in the 1930s, but were, mercifully, restored instead.

At the back of the house that was moved, are the remains of West Gate, one of the five gates which gave access to the walled city of Exeter. Two of West Gate's triumphant moments are recorded on a plaque. It was 'successfully defended against the rebel attacks in 1549', and 'William Prince of Orange, with his army entered the city in 1688 through this gate.'

But the gate itself, which was demolished in 1815, had little appeal for an early-nineteenth-century historian, who thought it 'a mean structure', and 'inferior in point of architecture to the other city gates.' It must have been, however, a welcome sight once to wayfarers who, having just crossed the eighteen-arch, thirteenth-century Exe Bridge, had, at Exeter, reached the end of a long and possibly hazardous journey from the west.

Having passed through the gate's pointed archway, which was surmounted by a low square tower, these travellers, now finding themselves within the city wall, had the choice of reaching the heart of the city through Stepcote Hill, or Westgate Hill (West Street) and Fore Street (called High Street until the alterations of 1778). In 1778 the second Exe Bridge was built, a little further west than the old one. That part of the city wall, with its church of All-Hallows-on-the-Wall, which stood on the site

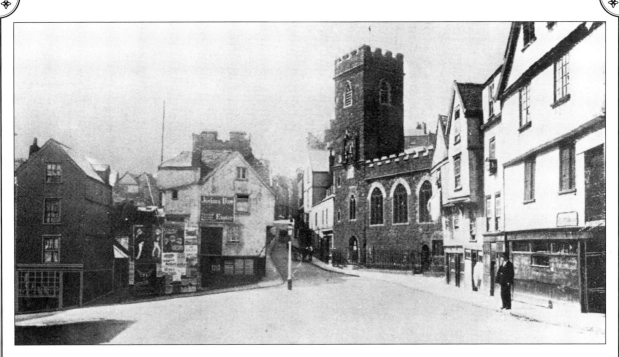

Part of 'The West Quarter', c.1900. West Street and St Mary Steps Church.

The same site since the 1970s.

Aerial view of the West Quarter taken around 1950.

Detail of the 'Matthew the Miller' clock.

Smythen Street and Butcher Row.

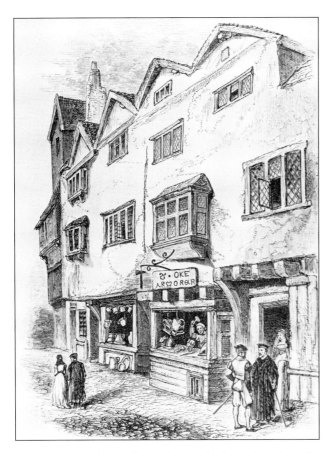

Frog Street as it was before its gradual erosion since the nineteenth century.

Frog Street with the eighteenth-century bridge of New Bridge Street. The Elizabethan house was demolished with Frog Street in the making of the inner by-pass. (J.W.)

between Bartholomew Street and West Street, was demolished in order to join the new bridge to High Street by building New Bridge Street. This opened a new and more convenient way into the city, but before this extensive work was carried out, the most direct route to its centre was Stepcote Hill leading to Smythen Street (the street of the smiths), Butcher Row, where indeed, as old prints show, there were many meat stalls, and to the upper part of South Gate Street. Preston Street, parallel to Stepcote Hill, and where in the sixteenth, seventeenth and eighteenth centuries rich merchants had gracious houses and large gardens, owes its name to the colony of priests who lived in that street before 1222. At that date, parish boundaries were defined and this enabled priests, eventually, to live within the parish of the church they served.

At one corner formed by West Street and Stepcote Hill, stands the church of St Mary Steps. Its real treasure is its Norman font which is probably contemporary with the mid-twelfth-century church which stood on the site before the present fifteenth century one was built. St Mary Steps being situated at the foot of a hill had to have its floor raised well above street level, and so it is reached from the main entrance by a flight of steps, hence its name, although it seems to have been called St Mary Minor once. Three bays of the lovely Devonshire screen belonged to the fifteenth-century chancel screen which was in

the medieval St Mary Major until that church was demolished in 1865. The rest of the screen at St Mary Steps is impeccably copied from the original and dates from the last century. The interior of the church was restored in 1866 and again 100 years later, when it acquired a new east window, but its style is that of the fifteenth-century Perpendicular.

The small door in its south wall is said to have once been used by the porter of the West Gate to reach a vaulted room which formed his living quarters, but the most popular attraction in this part of West Street, with The-House-That-Moved, is the unusual clock in the church tower.

It amuses visitors to watch its central figure nod his head with every stroke of the hour, and the two javelin men at his sides sound the quarters with their long hammers, on the bells at their feet. But whom do they represent? Was the clock made in the sixteenth century and does it really represent Henry VIII with two men-at-arms, as the serious-minded would have it? And did it receive its name of Matthew in affectionate memory of the dead miller of Cricklepit whose integrity and punctuality were legendary, when the clock was acquired by the church at the beginning of the seventeenth century? Or were the figures actually meant to represent Matthew the Miller and his two sons? And was the clock made in the early-seventeenth century by the

The House that Moved

Above: *Frog Street, c.1900.*
Right: *Frog Street with the famous house before its removal to West Street on 12 December 1961.*

The restored Frog Street house.

The Frog Street house 'firmly corseted with its wooden stays' on the way to its new site. (J.W.)

The installation of the house on the corner of West Street.

The house being hauled by Edmund Street.

locksmith and clockmaker Matthew Hopping who installed it and serviced it until his death in 1625? It is easier to be sure that the figures in the corners of the clock dial represent the four seasons!

The little square in front of St Mary Steps was formed some 15 years ago when a wide new road replaced the narrow one which skirted the medieval houses. The square was going to be paved for feet to walk on, but it has been tarmacked for wheels to park on. From here, as one looks towards the river, the protective narrowness of Edmund Street, Ewing Lane, Frog Street and Rackclose Lane is a memory; the reality is the tarmac barrenness of the new road system carrying its proliferating vehicles, and the sad colony of thin, overgrown lamposts. From this point the well-restored thirteenth-century bridge is not noticeable and the chunky ruin of St Edmund's tower seems irrelevant.

Sources
Sixteenth to nineteenth-century maps of Exeter
Nineteenth and twentieth-century newspaper reports
A. Jenkins's *History of Exeter*
Beatrix Cresswell's *Exeter Churches*
W.G. Hoskins's *Two Thousand Years In Exeter*

Exeter's thirteenth-century Exe Bridge as revealed since demolition of nearby buildings in the early 1970s.

CHAPTER 6

The Exe Bridges, The Shilhay and Exe Island

One of the two most inhuman areas in Exeter spreads across the river and is formed by wide, barren, depressing and bewildering roads which include the new, inelegant Exe Bridges. On these denuded sites once stood, on both sides of the river, streets and houses of various ages, and set at different angles, along which it was a pleasure to wander.

However, on the city side of the Exe, there are two redeeming features: one is old; the other is new.

The substantial remains of the first Exeter Exe Bridge made of stone, have been well restored and their surroundings agreeably landscaped. Unfortunately, the level of the dismal new roads is so much higher than that of the original street pattern that this most attractive spot is hardly noticeable from the motorway-like lanes which surround it. To enjoy a good view of the thirteenth-century bridge in its pleasing setting, one should walk up to New Bridge Street and stand on the bridge which spans Frog Street.

The other redeeming feature of the area is the recently built Shilhay housing estate. The new houses stand between two now piped leats which, in the past, as open channels, supplied power to the mills of the area. These leats are Lower Leat on the Commercial Road side, and Coney Lake on the river side.

Whether seen as a whole from Commercial Road or from the Exe Bridges, the Shilhay estate creates a pleasing overall effect. This was revealed even as the houses were being built, but to appreciate the trouble the architects (Warren & Taylor) must have taken so that the general aspect of the new estate would be in harmony with its older environment, the Shilhay houses have to be seen from the other side of the river. They fit in perfectly with the dominant colours and shapes of the buildings on the rising slopes that form the background. At a lower level, and nearer than the new houses, the grass bank and river are a most suitable foreground. Viewed sideways, from the Quay, near the ferry, between the skyline formed by the hills above Barley House, and the river below ground level, the new Shilhay looks like a fascinating old village.

The houses of the Shilhay estate are cleverly arranged at attractive angles around unevenly shaped courtyards whose names aptly recall the ancient woollen trade, 'Shearman Court', 'Weavers Court', 'Dyers Court'. These houses are also of slightly different height and width, and their windows are neither identical nor in the same position in all the buildings. This is most successful in preventing monotony, and so are the various roof lines. We can enter the several courts separately from Commercial Road (and they have access to the riverside too), but they also communicate, each with its neighbours, through passages of different shape and width, some supported by brick pillars. All this variety forms a most exciting townscape.

Much attention has also been given to texture, colour, and other details. The range of shades (from light to dark grey) of the concrete tiles from the Midlands, used on all the roofs and on the walls of alternate houses, is most successful in creating the same effect as that of happy weathering on good quality slates. The local bricks from Westbrick Ltd have an attractive uneven shade of dark red to purple, and a rough texture, which is emphasised by the neat and well-recessed pointing between them. All this blends admirably with the walls of converted warehouses nearby.

The curving wall in one court; the grass bank in another, separating a parking place from a footpath at a higher level; and the iron railings with fluted posts, are all imaginative details. So are the diagonally placed slats which surround the frontdoors' glass panels; the pleasingly curved ends of brick slopes and steps; and the good paving of concrete slabs incorporating a mixture of pebbles.

As we emerge from Shearman Court into the open and look to the south, we have a delightful view of the river, of the Quay with its attractive warehouses and cellars, and above the cliff, of the lovely Colleton Crescent.

We owe the first Exe Bridge made of stone, at Exeter, to Walter Gervase who was mayor of the city four times between 1218 and 1239. He is said to have started a fund to raise money to build a bridge because people who forded the river, which was then wider, shallower and tidal, were sometimes drowned.

Gervase's bridge, which had 18 arches alternately pointed and round, crossed the river diagonally, covering the distance almost from the West Gate to a point at which also ended, on the St Thomas side, the 1904 bridge which was recently demolished. Much of this thirteenth century bridge was over marshes where the tide flowed back and forth. Now that the buildings which covered it have been demolished, we can see eight of its arches and part of another. The bridge was made of the volcanic stone quarried in

Exeter's second stone 'Exe Bridge' built 1778, demolished 1903.

Northenhay near Rougemont Castle, and the church of St Edmund was built over two of its arches. But the thirteenth-century church was almost entirely rebuilt in 1832 and 1854, and in 1833 the bridge had been widened from 16¹/₂ft. to 33ft. by the extension in brick of its stone arches. This total width supported Edmund Street, then the main road to the west, until a few years ago. The removal of the nineteenth-century addition to the structure, and its restoration, enable us to see this part of the thirteenth-century bridge very much as it was originally.

After weirs were constructed in the thirteenth and fourteenth centuries, and leats were made to drain the land (and also to supply water power) the river became narrower and deeper (and it was no longer tidal). So the second stone bridge, which replaced the thirteenth century one in the eighteenth century, was much shorter. It crossed the river in a straight line from New Bridge Street, which was made then (above Exe Island) to join Fore Street to the new bridge. But only the section of the old bridge which spanned the river was demolished, the part which had been mostly over the marshes remained, and a short road was made to link it to New Bridge Street and the new bridge. This road was called, when later it was lengthened across the Shilhay, City Road; later still, it was renamed Commercial Road.

The eighteenth-century bridge owed its existence to the steepness of the streets which linked the old bridge to the city centre and which by then had become a great inconvenience. But although the first stone of the new bridge was laid in 1770 and the building 'proceeded with great rapidity', as the almost completed structure collapsed in a flood, and there was some delay to recover the stones, appoint another architect and start the work again, the bridge was not finished until 1778.

Again at the beginning of this century, contemporary conditions prompted the decision to build another Exe Bridge, and so the fine eighteenth-century stone bridge was replaced in 1904 with an

Exeter's third 'Exe Bridge', erected 1904, lasted some 70 years.

The latest Exe Bridge.

elegant steel structure. It lasted some 70 years and the reason for its demolition was that it made conditions worse in times of floods as water reached the top of the arch.

If we go towards Commercial Road from the Custom House, we walk across Quay Bridge which spans two leats; they join just before reaching the bridge and are called Higher Leat and Lower Leat. Past the bridge, we come to the Shilhay, once the centre of activity for Exeter's woollen trade and now with the new estate. Quay Bridge itself probably dates from the late-seventeenth century when the Elizabethan quay was improved and the Custom House was built. This bridge gave access directly to rackfields, but by the late-eighteenth century, here was also a quay used to unload coal, as shown by contemporary maps.

Exeter had a thriving woollen trade for some 350 years. From the city, the wool was sent to villages outside where it was spun and woven. Then, as material it was returned to Exeter where it was washed (to get rid of the fatty substance in the wool called lanolin) and dyed. These operations took place in the fulling mills. In the Shilhay, they were operated by water power supplied by the leats (water channels cut in the Bonhay area) which rejoined the river after going under Quay Bridge.

Once washed and dyed the material was put outside on racks to dry, and the open spaces where rows of these large wooden frames stood were called rackfields. Naturally they had to be close to the fulling mills. As an Exeter plan of 1723 shows, the Shilhay had large rackfields which spread across the site where, over 100 years later, Commercial Road would be built.

'Tenter', a word of Latin origin, was sometimes used instead of 'rack', which is derived from the Anglo-Saxon. And so, L-shaped nails called tenterhooks and used to hold the material to the tenter, while it is drying in a stretched position, gave us the expression 'to be on tenterhooks'.

Before the road was made, the area was divided between Great Shilhay and Little Shilhay by a leat called Coney Lake (the word 'lake' here derives from the Anglo-Saxon 'lacu' meaning a stream or water channel). It was cut near Exe Bridge and rejoined the

Aerial view of the River Exe and Bridge, c.1950.

river opposite the old quay, close to Quay Bridge. All the land on the river side of Coney Lake formed the Great Shilhay, and the site north of Coney Lake up to the city wall was Little Shilhay. The origin of the name, whose spelling varies ('Shilley' in 1723) is probably geological, 'shilly' or 'shelly' meaning gravel, shingle, pebble, and 'shillet' being a dialect word for shale. The upper rock layer in the Shilhay is formed by gravel, sand and shale.

Coney Lake was piped in 1967, and now runs, unseen, on the river side of the new Shilhay houses. When it was free, the little bridges over it, which linked the back of the old Commercial Road houses to the Great Shilhay, gave this spot a very picturesque aspect.

There are in this now-derelict area, early-eighteenth century buildings which must have once been used as mills and which probably replaced the much older, original buildings on the site. If we start from the back of the Custom House and follow a narrow path (once called Rack Close Lane) at the foot of the city wall, we can still see Higher Leat. Further down, and parallel to it, was the now-piped Lower Leat. They worked the corn and fulling mills in the Shilhay.

The Bishop Blaize Inn in Commercial Road also recalls the woollen trade. It was once a meeting-place for its freemen and apprentices, and the back of the building, with its cobbled ground, shows traces of the past. Bishop Blaize, a fourth-century martyr who had been tortured by having his flesh torn with a woolcomber's rake became the patron saint of weavers.

Nearby, the truncated Ewings Lane can still be seen. It led to Edmund Street (which no longer exists) at a point exactly opposite Frog Street. These streets were on a human scale, and it was fascinating to learn their history as one wandered through them observing their revealing details. Their site, now depressingly denuded, has been raised in a vast platform of wide and confusing crossroads.

The Shilhay remained Exeter's modest industrial estate until Marsh Barton began to be developed after the First World War. The part of it situated to the north of Commercial Road, with what remains of its leats, old buildings and cottages, might have been cleaned up and restored, and it could have become an industrial archaeologist's paradise, as well as an attraction for the citzens of Exeter and their visitors.

After the Prayer-Book Rebellion, in 1549, the Earl of Devon was deprived of his manor of Exe Island, which was then given to the citizens of Exeter by the king to reward their support.

It was Higher Leat and Lower Leat which made

The destruction of the Exe Bridge.

Detail of the destroyed bridge.

The removal of bridge sections.

this land an island by enclosing it. Like the Shilhay, it had once been part of a vast marsh which served as a natural defence on the south-western side of the city. Lower Leat, now piped, flowed under the church of St Edmund, and until some 15 years ago, one could see Higher Leat running alongside the alley way at the rear of the West Street houses. It can still be seen from New Bridge Street flowing under an eighteenth-century bridge and in Exe Island, at the back of Tudor House in Tudor Street.

Exe Island has one gem: the beautifully-restored Tudor House which is the subject of another chapter in this book. Other buildings are dull and depressing to look at. Yet, before its insensitive reconstruction, the place had charm. Old Frog Street led to it and was marvellous in itself. It had retained its original width and shape although only the house which formed the corner with Edmund Street (and which was moved further up the street in 1961) was very old, dating from the early-fifteenth century. Further on, though, on the other side of Frog Street, there was a fine Elizabethan house.

But there were intriguing relics of a less distant past exactly opposite the house which was moved: two old shop windows with nineteenth-century lettering on glass (which should have been preserved). In December 1961 it was still possible to read on one of the glass panels, that the place had been the 'Pioneer Coffee Tavern, West Gate', and this was illustrated with a picture in gold and colour of the West Gate surrounded by flamboyant scrolls. Another glass panel, with similar lettering, announced, 'Hot dinners daily from 12 to 3 6d. and 8d. chops steaks and soup.'. Available also were 'tea, coffee, cocoa and all kinds of summer and winter drinks', and the glass panel of the entrance door revealed that upstairs there was a 'lecture Room'.

The coffee tavern had been established by the Pioneer Temperance Society in the 1880s with the object of doing social work among the young of the West Quarter and encouraging them to treat the tavern as a meeting-place. Many people then lived in tiny houses, some in courts off Frog Street, others in Ewings Lane. The men were mostly employed in or near the Shilhay.

In 1913 the tavern's lecture room was converted into a dormitory, and it seems that by then it had somewhat changed its character, becoming a lodging house, although it also remained a cafe until the First World War. It was closed as a lodging house in August 1961, and was then acquired, with the adjacent property, by the city council, in order to

View of the old industrial area of Shilhay after a snowfall, c.1962.

A remaining feature of Exeter's industrial past in the Shilhay.

Workers in the Bodley Foundry, once in the Shilhay.

The successful new Shilhay estate seen from St Thomas's.

Part of the new Shilhay Estate, 1979.

This illustrates how perfectly the new houses fit in with their older environment.

The houses of the new Shilhay Estate are cleverly arranged at attractive angles around unevenly shaped courtyards.

The Shilhay Estate. Details.

The Shilhay Estate. Details.

Leat Terrace showing cottages in well-kept condition and the Higher Leat, a source of power for the mills.

Leat Terrace and Higher Leat in later condition (now a car park).

Edmund Street showing below the road the 1833 brick extension to the arches of the medieval bridge.

Higher Leat flowing under the eighteenth-century bridge in New Bridge Street.

The 'Pioneer Coffee Tavern', West Gate, which was opposite the original site of the Frog Street House.

Exe Island entrance sign.

The 'Lodging House', Exe Island, demolished in the 1960s.

demolish it (March 1962) and to prepare the site for the new, wide soulless Frog Street which now seems to take the fast-moving traffic under a railway bridge. This is the insipid, brick-and-concrete replacement for the colourful, arched and buttressed eighteenth-century stone bridge which supported New Bridge Street and spanned Frog Street.

Until the early 1960s, after walking down the slightly curving and picturesque Frog Street, one would have suddenly faced the fine archway and pleasingly rugged buttresses of this bridge. Then, having gone through the archway, one would have reached an attractive enclosure in Exe Island.

The slate-hung house at right-angles to the dark-red Pocombe stone and white limestone bridge, whose flights of steps led to its elegant balusters in New Bridge Street, the Georgian houses, the brick-red Heavitree stone lodging house, all formed a delightful square. From it, a quaint passageway called Rosemary Lane led to Bonhay Road. Its site is somewhere under the forbidding glass-and-concrete structure which denies the past of Exe Island.

Sources
City Records
Maps of Exeter, 1587–1860
Alexander Jenkins's *History of Exeter*
W.G. Hoskins's *Two Thousand Years In Exeter*
English Dictionary on Historical Principle
Express & Echo, reports in February and March 1962

The Exe Island side of the eighteenth-century archway under New Bridge Street. (J.W.)

The 1960s replacement and Western Way which replaced the picturesque Frog Street.

The Tudor House after restoration, 1978.

CHAPTER 7

St Edmunds Square and Tudor House

There used to be in Exe Island, off Tudor Street, a delightful little enclosure called St Edmunds Square. Its brick cottages were structurally sound and faced attractive small gardens. Instead of modernising the cottages, the city council allowed their demolition. The site was filled with rubble and overgrown vegetation for a considerable number of years, but it has now been absorbed by the premises of a firm of engineering suppliers, which cover a vast area along Bonhay Road on either side of Tudor Street. St Edmunds Square stood on part of the site of this firm's large car park which is entered from Tudor Street.

In contrast, also in Tudor Street, stands Tudor House, a credit to the genius of its owner restorer, Mr Bill Lovell, who spent 12 years and a great amount of money on its splendid restoration.

Tudor House is a four-storey building whose attractive slate work covers the façade at first-floor level. According to a nineteenth-century architect, the whole façade was slate-hung until about 1820.

The house is double fronted, and a narrow passage gives access from the splendidly restored doorway of the entrance to a winding staircase which leads to two rooms at each floor level.

Mr Lovell completely rebuilt one ground-floor window, the bay windows of the second floor, and he

The house in poor condition in the early 1960s.

Timber and cob wall between two second-floor rooms. (J.W.)

Seventeenth-century Tudor House in about 1900.

45

St Edmunds Square in the 1950s.

(J.W.)

Site of St Edmunds Square in the 1970s (Tudor Street).

partly rebuilt those of the first floor, using old timber, and being guided for their shape by small marks left in the frames of the openings.

The plaster of the façade, between the ground floor and the slate work was removed, and the beautiful texture and colour of the original stone and brick work is now exposed. From the second floor, between the timber frame of the façade was cob (clay incorporating straw) covered inside and outside with plaster. In the course of the restoration the cob was replaced with metal lathing. This ensures strength without affecting the appearance. Some original cob can still be seen, however, between the arched brace and posts of the wall which divides the two second-floor rooms. The timber roof has original rafters, purlins and wooden pegs.

Tudor House does not belong to the Tudor period. It is undisputedly early-seventeenth century in style and probably dates from the 1630s. The deeds of the house state that it was 'erected by Isaac Burche the Elder'. He was a maltster, and died in 1683.

Thanks to documents in private hands, it has been possible to discover that the Gubbs family were the owners of Tudor House in the 1670s, and as it is recorded that John Gubbs married Elizabeth Leach in September 1670, there is little doubt that the impaled arms in the slate work above the entrance refer to this couple. The 'holy lamb passant' (on the left side facing the house) being the arms of the Gubbs family, and 'ermine three crowns in chief' (on the right side), those of the Leach family. The lion rampant, the arms on the far left of the house, could refer to the Northmores, who owned the property some time in the eighteenth century.

The arms of John Duntze, the merchant, are similar to those of John Gubbs, which explains the mistaken claim that Duntze lived at Tudor House. There is no truth either in the often repeated statement that Catherine Turberville and Simon Leach, who were married in about 1600, ever lived there.

The deeds of Tudor House reveal the sad story of Thomas Smith and his sisters to whom the house had been left in the mid-eighteenth century, but who had to sell it to settle the debts of their father from whom they had inherited it.

It was because the daughter of the man who bought the house from the Smiths, married Robert Trewman, that it eventually belonged to the proprietor of the famous newspaper, Trewman's *Exeter Flying Post*. His grandson sold the house in 1861, and it passed into various hands until it was bought in 1963 by Mr. Lovell.

Text based on personal observation at the time of the restoration of the building, and information received from the owner restorer, Mr Bill Lovell.
Documents: the deeds of the house, and others in the hands of a descendant of the Northmore family.

CHAPTER 8

Tuckers Hall

Tuckers Hall in Fore Street has a splendid interior, but only its timber roof belongs to the building, which was erected in the fifteenth century, the rest being altered later and, incredible as it may seem, the whole edifice threatened with demolition in 1853.

If it survives, it is thanks to a lack of money at the time, to demolish it and erect a new hall in its place. Ironically, it is often only to such a reason that we owe the survival until our own days of buildings of historical and architectural interest. Unfortunately, money can always be found nowadays by a local authority to acquire, demolish and rebuild (often in a big and inferior way).

The woollen trade in Exeter consisted at first of separate guilds connected with the various operations which contributed to produce the material. Then in the fifteenth century the three crafts of weavers, fullers (also called tuckers) and shearmen combined to form a single guild or corporation which was recognised as the Honourable Company of Weavers, Fullers and Shearmen by Royal Charter in 1479.

Tuckers Hall had been erected in 1471. It was really then a chapel dedicated to 'The Assumption of Our Lady', but it did not only serve as a place of worship for the members of the Company, it was also their meeting place where they could discuss business matters. The east end was used as a church and was separated by a partition from the western part which was reserved for business. The timber roof of Tuckers Hall, upstairs, dates from that period.

The spinners and weavers worked at home, mostly in villages outside Exeter, some weavers possessing only a single loom, others having several. The fulling, as we have seen in the chapter dealing with the Shilhay, took place mostly in that district of Exeter.

After the material had been cleaned, dyed and dried in the fulling mills and on the rackfields, another operation was carried out which consisted in shearing with special shears to cut off the irregularities of the material's edges, and burling irons were used to remove the knots (a burl is a knot). All this was the work of shearmen, and some of the implements they used can be seen today at Tuckers Hall.

At the head of the Corporation was the Master assisted by two wardens. Apprentices served seven years and then became Freemen. After this their election to higher offices within the Corporation depended on their combined ability and popularity.

The Chapel of The Assumption of Our Lady was confiscated on religious grounds at the time of the Reformation, but the Corporation was able to acquire it again in 1578. It was stripped of its religious character though, as the building was to become solely the Company's business headquarters. This is why the fifteenth century edifice was altered then. Instead of remaining like a church, a single-storey building, a whole floor was inserted dividing it into ground-floor and upper storey. Thus in the hall upstairs we can still see the original timber roof of the fifteenth-century chapel, but the chimney piece in this room dates from these alterations of the last quarter of the sixteenth century, and the lovely wood panelling belongs to the early-seventeenth century.

Exterior of Tuckers Hall, 1979, showing the neo-Gothic façade built in 1905.

Tuckers Hall showing the fifteenth-century barrel roof and seventeenth-century wood panelling.

Window of Tuckers Hall.

Detail of wood carving.

Spinning wheel in Tuckers Hall.

The carved arms of the Corporation, which are still there, contain two shuttles, a teasel, a pair of shears and two burling irons. These arms were granted by Queen Elizabeth in 1564, two weeks before she confirmed the arms of the city (the motto Semper Fidelis was granted 24 years later).

As for the ground floor of Tuckers Hall, from 1675 until the beginning of this century, it housed a school whose pupils were the sons of members of the Corporation of Weavers, Fullers and Shearmen.

The Company had annual events such as on the 24 June, the election of a new Master and of two Wardens. It coincided with the procession of all the city guilds whose representatives walked in order of seniority of their corporations. The weavers carried the effigy of their patron saint, Bishop Blaize, and his emblem, the woolcomber's rake. This was the instrument with which, in the fourth century, he had been martyred for his Christian faith.

Each year, on 15 August (the date was changed later to 5 November), a dinner was given in honour of the newly elected Master. But once a month meetings took place at Tuckers Hall at which workers were engaged; any aspect of business could be discussed; and material was inspected. Men who had produced inferior quality were fined for not conforming to specified standards. An entry in a minute-book of the Corporation records that after two members had gone to the Shilhay to inspect some woollen cloth, they had reported that it was on the racks 'newly burled' and 'shorn badlie'.

Exeter's woollen trade had its most flourishing period in the seventeenth and eighteenth centuries. It began to decline in the early-nineteenth century and by 1850 there was little of it left in the city. But other trades were invited to join the Company and this is why it still exists and its annual dinner still takes place.

Tuckers Hall had its interior well restored in 1905 and its façade was rebuilf in neo-Gothic style.

Source
Beatrix Cresswell, *The Short History of the Worshipful Company of Weavers, Fullers and Shearmen of the City and County of Exeter*

CHAPTER 9

No. 143 Fore Street and St John's Church (Wheaton's)

One of the distinctions of an early-eighteenth-century house in Fore Street is that it was neither damaged during the war nor threatened with demolition in recent times. This is No. 143 where, on occasion, Charles Dickens was a guest.

This house was both the home of Thomas Latimer and the premises where the printing of the *Western Times* was carried out from 1840. Latimer was at first its managing editor and eventually its proprietor. He and Dickens had met when they were reporting, from Exeter, the famous case of Dick Turpin, who had been accused of murdering a Moretonhampstead farmer.

It was when, later, the Fore Street house was also used as a clearing house for the distribution in the

Westcountry of the London newspapers' advance copies, that Dickens, then Editor of the *London Daily News*, called there on his way to, and back from Plymouth, before returning to London by the evening train.

This Queen Anne house – actually built early in the reign of George I – still has features such as a staircase with twisted balusters, a handrail gently curving upward at each turn, and a panelling following the same line, which are typical of the early-eighteenth century.

In the courtyard, once reached directly through a passageway from Fore Street, is a characteristic Queen Anne porch-hood, held by unadorned brackets. The hood shows a head surmounted by an

No. 143 Fore Street (Wheaton's) exterior, 1979.

arrangement of stylised leaves resembling the antlers of a deer. The windows in the courtyard, with their thick glazing bars, and flush with the wall, as well as the coved cornice of the roof, are also typical of the Queen Anne period. On the street side, the upper part of the façade still retains its original Queen Anne features: large keystones over the windows, a projecting central part, and thick, white corner-stones.

This house was built in 1717 for Sir Thomas Bury, an eminent merchant of Exeter. He owned several houses but this one was his favourite, probably because so much care had gone into its construction. The architect had even sent to Bath for joiners he considered skilled enough to make the window sashes, some of these being round-headed. There were tastefully laid-out gardens, and the whole property extended as far as Bartholomew Street. On this side was Thomas Bury's terrace walk from which, then, he would have enjoyed fine views of the river and of the Exwick hills. The ground floor of the house once comprised a spacious entrance hall, large dining and drawing-rooms, and a breakfast room. Up above were the seven principal bedrooms.

The names of James Duntze and Elizabeth could still be seen in the 1960s engraved on two of the old window panes. These were the names of two of Sir John Duntze's children. He was a wealthy wool merchant, and he and his family lived at the Fore Street house. Later, and until 1837, another Exeter merchant lived there, but undoubtedly the most colourful character to have inhabited No. 143 Fore Street was Thomas Latimer.

After he had settled in Exeter when still a young man, he turned down the offer of a post in London on the ground that 'If I went to London I should get more money but I should also spend it, while I should lose the pleasure of this beautiful scenery.'

Constructive suggestions for social improvements, and support for any quarter that recommended them, often appeared in his writing, which was sincere, but vitriolic when he encountered resistance to liberalism. It was the violence of his literary expression that cost him his job once and libel suits many times. His polemics made lively reading and his invectives, often directed at the Bishop of Exeter, shocked or entertained his readers.

In spite of his forceful criticisms of some members of the Church and contempt for any form of bigotry, he was a sinceiely religious man whose writings contributed to social progress in his time.

As for Wheaton's, as printers, publishers, bookbinders, booksellers and stationers, who eventually did much business in the county, they occupied No. 143 Fore Street in the early part of this century. The *Western Times* was still being published there until 1904, but by 1905 Wheaton's had moved in.

The business of bookselling had been started by William Wheaton who, by 1839 was established at No. 185 Fore Street (the corner with North Street), the present site of Cornish's the outfitters. The Wheaton premises had been sixteenth or seventeenth-century gabled houses, which were demolished when the present red brick Brock Cornish building was erected in 1884. Cornish's actually moved into their premises in 1905 when Wheaton's left.

Printing and publishing ceased at No. 143 Fore Street in the mid-1960s, but stationery was still available there until the end of that decade. Wheaton's was no longer a strictly local firm; most of the business was transferred to the industrial estate at Marsh Barton; and only a fraction of the large Fore Street premises was used as a bookshop.

As the window in Exeter Cathedral, which commemorated Thomas Latimer since 1889, was destroyed during the Second World War, the house at No. 143 Fore Street, once his home and place of work, is his only memorial. It also remains a credit to Thomas Bury's architect. But one wonders what its fate will be now that Wheaton's shop has closed down and the building is empty.

St John's Church

No doubt Thomas Bury, John Duntze, Thomas Latimer, and others who lived at No. 143 Fore Street, would have worshipped at St John's Church, which stood nearby but on the other side of Fore Street, at its junction with the very narrow John Street. St John's Church was demolished in three stages

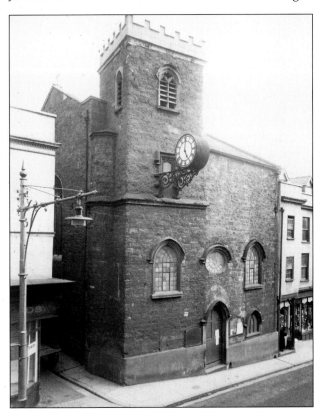

St John's Church, on the corner of Johns Street and Fore Street, c.1920.

Fore Street looking east, 1979.

Photo c.1900.

The interior of St John's Church.

between 1864 and 1957. It had been founded, it seems, in the eleventh century, but it is not clear whether it was dedicated to the Baptist or the Evangelist.

Like St Stephen's Church in High Street, St John's had its original chancel over an arch, which stood across John Street in this case. This was known as 'John's Bow'.

When street 'improvements' were alleged to be necessary, the Bow was inspected and conveniently considered unsafe. Then, it was reported that any money spent on repairing it would be wasted. So in 1864, the picturesque arch with the chancel of the church, was taken down, and a new east wall and chancel were built, thus reducing the length of the church.

A peculiarity of this building was that having come through a doorway on its Fore Street side at vestry level, one had to reach the interior of the church by going up a staircase. This apparently had been the arrangement, after alterations, since 1778 when Fore Street was lowered so as to connect by an easy gradient with the newly built Bridge Street (which led to the new bridge). Fore Street was lowered from St John's Church to its junction with West Street, and from this point, where the city wall was removed, arches were built down to the bridge, to support the new road.

So the level of the church on which the congregation had to attend its services after the eighteenth-century alterations, was actually 'upstairs'. As well as having pews, the little church had galleries on its

south and west sides, which had been erected to accommodate the parishioners of St George's Church when the latter was demolished in 1843.

After St John's Church had been made redundant three years earlier, it was pulled down in 1937, but its tower was kept as a monument of historic interest. Only for another 20 years though! In 1957, the Ministry of Works allowed its demolition. In accordance with what seems to be an Exeter tradition, the tower had been reported to the Ministry as being 'in a dangerous condition'! Before the tower was removed though, its famous lighted clock, which for several generations had hung over the street from a projecting bracket, had been taken down in an attempt to relieve the strain on the tower.

A reader of a local newspaper seems to have summed up the feelings people in the neighbourhood had had for this clock, when some 20 years ago he wrote, 'That drum clock had as friendly a face as the benignest of full moons and seemed to give a helping hand to pedestrians climbing the steep slope.'

Sources
R.S.Lambert, *The Cobbett of the West*
Devon & Cornwall Notes and Gleanings
Nineteenth-century directories
Nineteenth-century *Exeter Flying Post*
Nineteenth-century *Western Times*
Beatrix Cresswell (1908), *Exeter Churches*
Express & Echo, January 1937, February 1957, June 1972.

✦ CHAPTER 10 ✦

St Nicholas Priory

In Exeter, 'The Mint' is a confusing name, and a difficult place to find. It is a narrow, pedestrian way which joins Fore Street to Bartholomew Street, but bearing in mind the available documents in the city archives, one can say that it is most unlikely that there ever was a mint or an assay office in this lane.

As a complete thoroughfare 'The Mint' did not exist until after the Dissolution of St Nicholas Priory. Before that, the Priory's church, refectory and cloister were right across the site of the present lane.

In the early part of the eighteenth century, this narrow way was called Old Mint Lane and the name could refer to mints in nearby Friernhay or Mary Arches Street, which had functioned for a short time, and were respectively closed in the mid- and late-seventeenth century. Or the word 'Mint' could be – as the nineteenth-century Roman Catholic priest and scholar George Oliver thought – a contraction of the word minster and refer to St Nicholas Priory.

Before the Dissolution of the Priory in 1536, there had been a St Nicholas Lane, and part of its site coincides with part of the present lane. The main gate of the Priory, giving access to its grounds and buildings, was on the site of the junction of 'The Mint' with Fore Street. From this gate, St Nicholas Lane led to the west end of the church and to the western side of the cloister-entry, that is to the BACK of the building which is open to the public today, which in medieval times was its FRONT, and of course the entrance to all the monastic buildings and the cloister.

The building we now call St Nicholas Priory represents about a quarter of the original Benedictine Priory and it is possibly unique in this country as the complete western range of a medieval monastic establishment whose plan, devised to comply with monastic rule, is still almost intact.

At right-angles with this well-maintained building, on the other side of the lane, is what remains of the monks' refectory, and of a courtyard which is the site of the cloister, and which had retained some charm until the erection of a workshop was allowed there in 1970. The Priory church was opposite the refectory, forming the south side of the cloister, and opposite the western range, on the

St Nicholas Priory before restoration.

53

St Nicholas Priory as seen from the garden of No. 26 Bartholomew Street West.

The fifteenth-century Guest Hall showing the arch-braced roof.

eastern side of the cloister, were the warming-house, the chapter-house, and at first-floor level, the monks' dormitory. The cemetery was to the west of the church, on the Friernhay side of the grounds. At first, local wells supplied water, but from the fourteenth century an underground conduit brought spring water from the east side of the town to the Cathedral

Close and on to the Priory.

According to the *Chronicle of Battle Abbey*, compiled between 1066 and 1176, and whose original manuscript is in the British Museum, the foundation of St Nicholas Priory is connected with the church of St Olave. This is still in Fore Street, but although the present building is of much later date, it seems to incorporate some Saxon work in its fabric.

The church of St Olave was confiscated by William the Conqueror and given, with its land, to Battle Abbey, the monastery he had founded on the site of the Battle of Hastings, in Sussex.

Monks were sent from Battle to Devon to administer various lands which had been taken over, and one of these monks, Cono, was responsible for the church and land of St Olave. According to the *Chronicle*, he 'diligently applied himself to the enrichment and elevation of the place committed to his oversight.' Then, when he had accumulated a fair amount of property all round, he decided to build a monastery nearby. The *Chronicle* confirms that he succeeded in doing this and gives precisions, 'This he did by the license and authority of King William-the-Conqueror who was still living.' This wording seems to indicate that the foundation of St Nicholas Priory was in 1087, the last year of the Conqueror's life.

The Priory probably owes its dedication to another event which had taken place in 1087. It was the year when the remains of St Nicholas, the fourth-century Bishop, had been taken from Myra in Asia Minor, and brought to Bari in Southern Italy which was at the time occupied by the Normans. This news

This room was the Priors' Solar from the fifteenth century until the Dissolution. The plaster work dates from the late-sixteenth century. Note the unfortunate erection of barriers.

Part of the chimney piece once in the Vicars Choral Hall (South Street) showing the arms of Bishops Bantringham, Lacey, and Oldham. Now at the Priory.

was received with much jubilation throughout the Norman world and it is likely that William the Conqueror chose to dedicate his new priory in Exeter to this saint.

The building which can be visited and which was the Priory's western range, contained on the ground floor, the kitchen (once joined to the refectory but now divided from it by the width of the lane), and office called the cellarer's checker, the cellar (where all the provisions were kept), and the cloister-entry. The Prior's and guests' quarters were on the first floor, at opposite ends, and with access through different stairs. The guests would have been mostly travellers of some importance, and they would have taken their meals with the Prior in the guest-hall which was between their respective quarters.

From the fifteenth century, the guest-master's cell (which can still be seen) was at the top of the tower built then on the western side, and the lay-brothers'

The Undercroft.

quarters were above the kitchen. This floor was removed some 50 years ago, but the kitchen stair still leads to that level. On the way, we pass the doorway which was used by these lay-brothers to convey the food from the kitchen to the guest-hall.

Since the guests would not have been allowed in the cloister, there is no doubt that from the fifteenth century, when the western range underwent important alterations and the west tower was added, the guests' quarters were at the south end of the building, with direct access from the cloister-entry through their own staircase. So their dormitories were on two levels above the cloister-entry, the room which is now, we might say, back to front since its two doorways, that respectively lead to the present lane and to the small back garden, once gave access, the one to the cloister, the other from St Nicholas Lane and the grounds.

Much of the outside wall of the Priory building along 'The Mint', but not above first-floor level, dates from the Norman period. Some of the stones match perfectly the carboniferous shale of the Bonhay Road cliff, so they were probably quarried in that area. The cellar, a marvellous example of early-Norman architecture, has two massive pillars of limestone, and their original arches are formed by red and white sandstone. The wall with a fireplace in it, dates from the sixteenth century, when after the Dissolution the cellarer's checker was replaced by a larger room (used as an entrance hall today), which reduced the size of the cellar next to it. This we can see clearly by looking at the cellar arches, which are cut off on the fireplace side.

There were some alterations to the building in the thirteenth century, and again in the fifteenth when it was made higher. The kitchen dates mostly from the fifteenth century, but a window in it, now blocked, dates from the earlier alterations. The guest-hall upstairs retains thirteenth-century walls below its windows, and a thirteenth-century window in the

The exterior of St Nicholas Priory.

The Mint Lane with the Priory buildings on either side.

guests' dormitory, behind the fifteenth-century screen, shows that in the thirteenth century the guest-hall must have continued on this side beyond the point where it ends today. Otherwise, this room, with its fine arch-braced roof, windows on the garden side, fireplace and warming cupboard, is a splendid example of a fifteenth-century hall. The cloister-entry also shows two periods, having two Norman walls, and two thirteenth-century ones with pointed arches to their doorways.

The Priory buildings and grounds covered approximately 6½ acres, that is the area between Friernhay and Mary Arches Street, and that between Fore Street and Bartholomew Street, where the Priory's back gate was. This street name does not appear until 1637, but it was a busy, if narrow, thoroughfare in medieval times, just within the city wall, and leading from the North Gate to the West Gate.

Early in its life, an income was provided for St Nicholas Priory by St Olave's endowments, and the assets that Cono had acquired. Then the valuable royal gift of the church of Cullompton with its endowments, was added by Battle Abbey. An acknowledgement of subjection, on the part of St Nicholas Priory, took the form of a tax of 60 s. paid to Battle by the daughter house or 'cell'. This had risen to £7 at the Dissolution.

Cono became the first Prior of St Nicholas, but there does not seem to be any reliable source which mentions the number of monks who first came from Battle to serve the Priory, although an eighteenth-century writer states that it was six.

Adversity in the form of a fire which destroyed the new church before it was completed, was overcome when the place acquired fame for its miracles and attracted generous pilgrims whose gifts were not only sufficient to rebuild the church, but also 'to construct buildings for the residence of the brethren who dwelt there in charge of it.'

The Priory received numerous grants of land and other gifts throughout the twelfth and thirteenth centuries. Some of this land was as far as Ireland, and it could explain the origin of the Celtic shaft of a cross now in the Priory garden, which was found in a cut-water of the old Exe Bridge when it was demolished in the eighteenth century, but which is supposed to have been at St Nicholas Priory before the Dissolution. This section of an ancient high shaft, probably dating from the eighth century, has carvings very similar to those of the eighth century south cross at Ahenny (Tipperary). One design is identical on both shafts.

The Priors of St Nicholas Priory were chosen by the Abbots of Battle Abbey and presented to the Bishop of Exeter who confirmed the appointment and received an oath of obedience from the new Prior. The Priory was also subject to visitation by the Bishop. Nevertheless, the relationship between them was at times strained as shows the episode concerning frequent bell-ringing at the Priory which Bishop Osbern wanted drastically reduced, until Archbishop Anselm intervened in 1102 and a compromise was reached. And there was the dispute, a little earlier, over the monks' right of burial in their own cemetery, which the Bishop had questioned. This had to be settled by a letter to the Bishop from Pope Pascal himself, who upheld the monks' right to bury their dead in their own precinct. Trouble due to noisy dogs at the Priory, and to the obstinacy of the Prior in wanting to keep them, was something that Bishop Brantyngham had to contend with in the late-fourteenth century.

There were also disagreements between the Priory and the city authorities. One of them resulted in an arbitration, after which the site between the city wall and Bartholomew Street, down to Bartholomew Terrace, was awarded to the city chamber although the Priory had claimed it too.

St Nicholas Priory was surrendered by its last Prior, William Cullompton, in 1536. The church was demolished, but the domestic buildings remained and the eastern range probably survived until the new Roman Catholic Church of St Nicholas was erected on the site in 1790. This interesting neo-Norman building is still there but has not been used as a church since 1884.

After the Dissolution, the precinct and domestic buildings of St Nicholas Priory were sold by the Crown, and they were eventually acquired by the Mallet family. But it is probable that William Hurst (not the Mayor but his grandson) had the western range on a long lease by the 1580s and that it was he who had it modernised in the Elizabethan fashion of the day. The plaster ceiling of the present entrance hall, its doorway from the street and its east window opening, the plaster decorations in the room above (once the Prior's solar), the frescoes on the reveals of the fifteenth-century windows in the guest-hall, are all part of the late-sixteenth-century alterations. The initials W.M.H. in the ceiling at the bottom of the main staircase would refer to William Hurst and his wife Mary.

The Priory buildings and precinct were eventually divided and became the property of various people who, in the course of the centuries, filled in much of the open space.

Elias Cosserat, Master of the Corporation of Weavers Fullers and Shearmen, and his family, seem to have been, in the late-eighteenth century, the last people to occupy the old western range of the Priory as the fine residence that it had been for some 200 years. In 1804, it was described as 'now in a ruinous state.'

One of the subsequent owners sold part of the fair-sized garden, where in about 1820 the brick house of No. 26 Bartholomew Street was erected and a wall was built, which reduced the Priory garden to its present size.

When in 1913 the city council, influenced by its Town Clerk H. Lloyd Parry (who had contributed several works on Exeter's historical and architectural heritage) and acquired (for £850) the old Priory building to restore it, it had belonged to the Wilcocks, a family of bankers and merchants, for almost 100 years. By then the building had been split up into five lots of premises which had all been given entrance doors and new windows. Traces of these can still be seen in the restored walls.

These premises were occupied by a bootmaker, an upholsterer, and there was a small physical training centre for the youths of the district in the present entrance hall. The marks made by the trapeze ropes in the soft Beer stone can still be seen near the apex of the Tudor arch. The guest-hall had become a creche where working mothers could leave their babies during the day. But the fifteenth-century kitchen converted into a three-storey house, and the flat formed within the Prior's old quarters, were never the slums they are supposed to have been; they were occupied by most respectable families.

The restoration of the building was skilfully carried out by a local architect, Lewis Tonar, under the supervision of Harold Brakspear, the highest authority on monastic architecture at the time. It was opened to the public in 1916 and curators were in charge of it until 1973.

The present status of St Nicholas Priory is that of a small museum, and it is excellent as such in its presentation of interesting sixteenth- and seventeenth-century objects. But what is to be regretted is that the architectural and historical significance of the Priory, Exeter's most outstanding ancient monument after the cathedral, is hardly conveyed by the notices which give information about the exhibits, and that nothing is said of the important relationship between the plan of this building and the life of its occupiers during its monastic period. In fact, certain original functions have been quite wrongly attributed to some of the rooms. Also, the erection of barriers in the kitchen, which spoil the visual effect and must have damaged the fifteenth-century floor, is deplorable.

Sources

The Chronicle of Battle Abbey
The deeds relating to St Nicholas Priory in the Record Office (Exeter)
George Oliver (1846), *The Monasteries of the Exeter Diocese*
Transactions Devonshire Association (Records of St Nicholas Priory,
Kate Clark (1912), *The Property of the Dissolved Monasteries*, Joyce Youings, 1952
Deeds relating to No. 26 Bartholomew Street West in Record Office.
Local newspaper reports 1913–16 relating to the purchase and restoration of St Nicholas Priory, and later eye-witness accounts.
The St Nicholas Priory scrapbooks of Maud Tothill (first Curator of the Priory)

St Olave's Church, Fore Street, c.1910.

CHAPTER 11

The Church of St Olave

There is no historical doubt about the connection between St Nicholas Priory and the original church of St Olave, which stood on the site of the present one in Fore Street. The evidence is in original records. However, who founded the church, when precisely, and to which of two saints of the same name it was dedicated, is not known. It can only be conjectured.

This church might have been founded towards the end of the reign of King Canute who died in 1035, and dedicated to Olaf Haraldson, the Norwegian king whose ardent Christianity after baptism replaced the Viking pirate expeditions of his adolescence, and who, after his death in 1030 while trying to reconquer his kingdom, acquired great fame as a saint although he was not canonised, and whose burial place at Trondheim became a place of pilgrimage. However, it has been objected that this dedication to 'Saint' Olaf or Olave would have been unlikely then, since Canute and his Danes had conquered Olaf's kingdom in 1028, and it was in a battle against the Danes that Olaf was killed.

Gytha, the mother of King Harold, endowed the church of St Olave in 1053 with the income from her manor of Sherford (in South Devon) and it has been suggested that St Olave's Church might even have been her own foundation. But the objection to this theory is again, if the dedication was to the Norwegian Olaf, that Gytha was Danish by birth. Another conjecture is that the church owes its dedication to a Welsh saint, St Gwynllyw of Gwent whose name was translated in English into 'Olave'!

What can be said with certainty is that the church of St Olave, which had been endowed before the Norman Conquest by Gytha, was given with its revenues by William the Conqueror to his foundation

St Olave's Church, Fore Street, 1979.

at Battle; that monks from the Abbey while taking care of the Exeter property, and with the authorisation of the king, began to build St Nicholas Priory; and that Battle Abbey transferred St Olave's and its endowments to its daughter house, the new priory at Exeter.

St Olave's was part of the precinct of the Priory and served as the parish church. It was rebuilt in the fourteenth century with the volcanic stone from the Northernhay area, and in this it differs from most of the other small churches in Exeter, which were re-erected in the fifteenth century, and in the construction of which Heavitree stone, a coarse standstone, was used. Its tower, unusually, is on the south side, and this may have had something to do with the situation of the church which was part of the boundary of the St Nicholas grounds. Until the last century, when the south wall of the church was rebuilt (using the original stones) in a position which is almost level with the outer wall of the tower, the latter protruded from the main body of the church far more than it does today.

There is, as we can see outside, partly forming the north-west corner of the main body of the church, long and short stones used consecutively, which could have come from the pre-Conquest building. The present windows are fifteenth century in style (Perpendicular).

Inside the church, what must have been a complete staircase within the tower, now leads to the pulpit. The nave and its adjoining north aisle have four bays and are divided by three octagonal columns of Northernhay stone whose ribbed capitals are fairly plain. The added aisle on the north side has only two bays and between the two aisles is one octagonal column of Beer stone. The original piscina,

also of Beer stone, can still be seen on the south side of the sanctuary. On the north side, the narrow, Northernhay stone staircase (now blocked) shows where the screen and rood used to be.

St Olave's Church is described in the early-nineteenth century as having next to its tower, a circular staircase leading over a gateway to a small chamber used by the sexton, which was once a room for the priests who served the church. There is no sign of this now.

After the Reformation, the church was closed for a considerable time, and when after the revocation of the Edict of Nantes in 1685, Protestant refugees left their native France to settle in Exeter, the Bishop put St Olave's at their disposal so that services there could be conducted in their own language. This went on for some 70 years during which time five Huguenot pastors served the church.

But the French colony, over the years, having been completely integrated, and English being no longer a language problem, there was by the 1760s no need for a French church in Exeter.

St Olave's was closed once more, and in the early-nineteenth century an historian noted, 'It is dark, gloomy, and as divine service is not performed in it little attention is paid either to cleanliness or interior repairs.'

The church was restored and reopened as a church of England parish church in 1815, and at the present time some services are still held at St Olave's.

Sources
Chronicle of Battle Abbey.
Devon Notes & Queries (*Exeter Churches*, Beatrix Cresswell, 1908–09)
Alexander Jenkins (1806), *History of Exeter*

CHAPTER 12

The Chevalier House

At the top of Fore Street, just above the market, and approximately on the site of the present Winstons Restaurant, stood a fine pair of seventeenth-century gabled houses whose façades displayed a profusion of timber. They were Nos 78 and 79 Fore Street. The latter was also known as the Chevalier House, after the small equestrian statue that stood on the ridge of its gable, but sometimes, with less precision, the name was applied to both houses.

These four-storey buildings were very similar, although No. 78, thought to date from about 1610, was said to be some 30 years older than its companion. At first and second-floor levels, they had mullioned bay windows, supported by carved corbels below which, at the higher level, could be seen oak posts forming equal panels all along the

width of both houses.

It is ironical that these two buildings, which in 1929 rallied so many individuals and organisations, against their possible demolition; which were saved thanks to the efforts of the local authority and the financial help of the central government; should have been destroyed (during an air raid) only 13 years later. This was 17 years short of 1959 when the city council would have totally repaid the government's loan and owned the houses!

For a considerable time in the last century, this property was owned by the Sercombe family, who came from Dunsford. But it was let by the mid-nineteenth century to J. Trehane, a wine and spirit merchant, who left his business to his son. The shops of both houses were then used by that firm, which remained there until the late 1880s. Then, Charles Ham, a wine and spirit merchant and mineral water manufacturer, who had rented these business premises, finally bought the property. Although various tenants, all wine and spirit merchants, had, in turn, their business there, Ham seems to have owned the houses until 1923, when they were bought by Carr & Quick Ltd, also in the same trade.

The reason why these two beautiful houses were threatened with demolition 50 years ago is that Woolworth, which had occupied the site next to them for five years, wanted to enlarge their premises, and to build the extension in the style of the day. So they made an offer of £20,000 for the pair, to Carr & Quick,

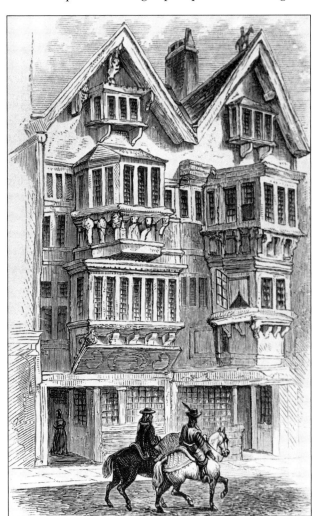

Reconstructed scene of the seventeenth century.

The small equestrian statue on the gable of the Chevalier Inn, No. 79.

61

Pre-war view of the Old Chevalier Inn.

with a view to demolishing them. 'Is Exeter to allow one of the most picturesque features of her principal thoroughfare to be swept away without a protest?' asked a reader in the *Express & Echo* on 16 October 1929, after that newspaper had discovered, and reported two days earlier what was afoot.

But among others, The Society for the Protection of Ancient buildings, and The Exeter Diocesan Archaeological and Architectural Association pleaded for the retention of the houses, and the city council's Finance and Estates Committees met promptly to see what steps could be taken to save them. The trouble was that at the time, although the council had the power to control the height of buildings being erected within the city, it had no power to stop an owner of property from pulling it down!

Fortunately, as in the case of Bampfylde House, the generous owners of the two Fore Street houses, so that they could be preserved, accepted to sell them to the city for half the price they had been offered by the

business firm. The city applied for a loan of £10,000 – oddly to us, to the Ministry of Health – and after a Ministry Inspector had come down to Exeter and made a favourable report, this was granted. The property was leased (at an annual rent of £600) by the council to Carr & Quick, for 30 years, this also being the period during which the loan had to be repaid to the Government.

After the decision to buy the buildings had been made, the *Devon & Exeter Gazette* observed, 'The city is fortunate in not only acquiring the property, but in having substantial proof that citizens will sink mercenary considerations when public interests are at stake.'

As for Woolworth, by 1934 it had moved to its present High Street site, occupied until two years earlier by Garton & King, the domestic engineers, and iron and brass founders, who, however, kept their Waterbeer Street premises for another four or five years. This is where their foundry was and the

Interior of The Chevalier showing oak panelling of walls and decorated ceiling.

The interior of The Chevalier.

site to which Woolworth extended in the mid-1970s. By 1936, Woolworth's first premises, in Fore Street, were occupied by the Exeter Corporation Electricity Undertaking, and four years later, the two seventeenth-century houses next to them became The Old Chevalier Inn.

Descriptions of these houses, which appeared in 1923 when they were for sale, and again in 1929–30, when the city was acquiring the property, show that many original features were still part of their interiors. There was at the time a bookshop (run by a Mr J.A. Martin) on the ground-floor of No. 79. This had been the entrance-hall and living room of the seventeenth-century occupants of the house. The panelling had been painted over, but this room still opened upon the original winding oak staircase, leading to the first-floor ornate drawing-room. Here the oak panelling covered the walls from floor to ceiling, and the windows' mullions still showed the marks of the adze with which they had been shaped.

In this room, between a massive oak beam and the cornice, there was a decorative plaster ceiling with ribs forming a geometrical pattern, and clusters of scrolls. No. 78 also had an original winding staircase, as well as some original oak panels and mullions on the upper floors. These respective premises did not only adjoin, but in parts they actually overlapped.

In one of the second-floor rooms of No. 79, there had been an oak cupboard let into the wall, at the back of which was a sliding panel that, on being moved by the initiated, revealed a secret chamber. This dark and narrow sanctuary, where someone in hiding might be concealed, was formed by a space under the steps of the staircase leading to the third floor. Later, a door replaced the chest, and on opening it the 'secret room' could be shown as a curio.

This, the actual Chevalier (or Cavalier) house was said to have been used as headquarters by Prince Charles (later Charles II), from September 1644 when,

in command of the army of the west, he had come to Exeter – which had been under the Royalists for a year. There does not seem to be any historical evidence that this house was ever used by Prince Charles. But it is possible that when in 1644 the King stayed at Bedford House; the Prince at the Deanery; and 'noblemen and others were lodged in the houses of the principal citizens who entertained them with great hospitality', some of these followers were accommodated at the Fore Street house and that after their departure the little equestrian statue was placed on the roof of the house to commemorate this visit and the King's and Prince's stay in the city. Exeter was not regained by the Parliamentary forces until April 1646.

A legend was told about the roof statue – which survived until the destruction of the two houses in the air raid: The forces of General Fairfax had surrounded the city for four months and the Royalist garrison looked in vain for help. By March the situation was very grim and the end of Royalist resistance approaching. And so, in remembrance of these sad days, every night in March, every year since 1646, the equestrian figure was said to leave its post and gallop to the top of the cathedral towers to watch over what were once the meadows of St Leonard's where the threatening army of Fairfax had been encamped!

Sources
City archives (deeds relating to 78/79 Fore Street)
Alexander Jenkins (1806), *City of Exeter*
Richard Izacke (1681), *City of Exeter*
Sir Edward Walker (1705), *Historical Discourses Upon Several Occasions*
Reports in *Western Morning News*, February 1923
Reports in *Express & Echo*, October and December 1929
Reports in *Devon & Exeter Gazette*, October 1929, January and February 1930
Besley's Directories from 1853 to 1940

Nineteenth-century St Mary Arches Street.

Mary Arches Street, 1979.

CHAPTER 13

Mary Arches Street and Bartholomew Street East

Until the late 1950s, Mary Arches Street had preserved some of its interesting and picturesque medieval pattern. Past the church, on its way to Bartholomew Street, Mary Arches Street suddenly curved to the left and narrowed to its original width. It has since been widened because it was thought once that buses would be routed that way. They were not, but the new width proved convenient later for the cars awaiting their turn to enter the car park!

In May 1942, Mary Arches Street was badly damaged in an air raid, and some reconstruction was unavoidable. To this we owe the two dull brick buildings which curve their dreary way round two sides of the junction of this street with Fore Street.

Next, on the western side, the well-maintained White Lion is, pleasingly, the retained, although modified, nineteenth century building. Adjoining it, a small square, St Olave's Close, is formed by one side of the White Lion; a brick wall whose sturdy stone base probably belonged to one of St Nicholas Priory's buildings; and a small single-storey factory.

This is a pleasant enough new building, but it is a pity that it owes its existence to the demolition of St Olave's Square, which had lost some of its houses in the air raid; whose remaining eighteenth-century cottages were neglected and needed modernising; but which still had much charm and which, rebuilt, could have been as attractive as it had been once and very convenient for people to live in. Access to St Olave's Square was through an alleyway whose entrance was in Fore Street, and which ended at the square with an archway.

This can still be seen beside the White Lion in St Olave's Close, and so can part of the alleyway, whose red sandstone wall has been plastered over, but which an eighteenth-century building still spans in a picturesque bridge effect. The nineteenth-century warehouse beside the archway helps to retain a little of the past atmosphere of this site.

The entrance to the church was once through its south door. This was within a yard divided from the street by iron rails and a gate. This yard had been used for burials, as a grave stone still shows. The church of St Mary Arches suffered much in the air raid; its walls were damaged; and its lovely barrel roof was completely destroyed. The church was reopened temporarily, and rededicated in 1950 after repair work had been carried out for several years. The work was completed in 1954 and its cost was met with a fund that had been raised by public appeals. For the restoration of the roof, oak and red pine were used which came from an American barge that had taken part in the Normandy landings of the last war, and which was broken up at Topsham.

St Mary Arches was a civic church, being the ancient parish church of the Guildhall. Most of its exterior is rather spoilt by the pointing and by the artificial stone that was used instead of red Heavitree sandstone, which would have suited better the Perpendicular style it acquired in the fifteenth century.

St Mary Arches Church.

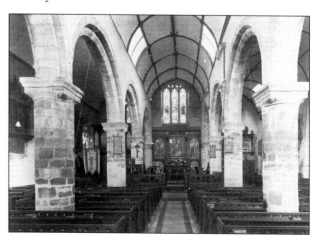

Interior of St Mary Arches Church, pre-war. Severely damaged in the bombing, its roof has been replaced but it retains the original Norman pillars.

The grounds of St Olave's Rectory, Mary Arches Street, 1979.

The garden of St Olave's Rectory, with the original refectory of St Nicholas Priory in the background.

The Norman interior dates from the twelfth century. Its cylindrical piers are surmounted by scalloped capitals and square abaci, and its round arches form four bays. At the east end, outside, we can see the width of the church as it was originally before aisles were added in the late-twelfth century, and later extended. St Mary Arches has exceptionally fine sixteenth- and seventeenth-century wall memorials.

Next to the church and forming the corner of a narrow lane, there is a new, modestly sized office block. Its corner windows, the texture and shade of its red bricks, the vertical use of their length on their narrow side, under the windows, in a chamfered effect, and its pillar-supported corner entrance, make this three-storey building rather attractive. But on its site stood a group of fine gabled houses; they could have been modernised and let to people to live in.

The narrow way at the corner of which is the new building was called George Lane. According to an early-nineteenth-century historian, it was once complete, leading to North Street through the George Inn yard. But long before his time, the lane had been cut off by buildings. However, probably since the erection of the Gaumont Cinema (now a bingo hall)

The erection of the Gaumont Cinema. This site was originally occupied by the George Inn and its yard.

some 50 years ago, it has been possible to reach North Street again through this lane and an open courtyard. The George Inn and its yard probably were on part of the site occupied by the bingo hall or its forecourt. In George Lane, is the Synagogue. It was built in 1764, and referred to in the early-nineteenth century as 'a small, plain, but neat edifice'.

The space between Mary Arches Street and North Street was gradually filled with houses, courtyards and alleyways which, by the nineteenth century formed an intricate pattern. But until the end of the sixteenth century the houses had been mostly along the line of the streets, the land at the back having remained open space. Apart from the church, there was in Mary Arches Street an important building which had probably been erected in the mid-fifteenth century. It was the Great House.

It was bought with its garden by John Maynard in the seventeenth century for £600 and there in 1662 he founded The Blue Maids Hospital 'for the maintenance and education of a certain number of poor girls.' This building which is represented on a sixteenth-century plan of the city with a massive tower flanked by walls which reach the upper floors of adjoining two-storey houses, is described over 200 years later as 'an ancient house with a battlemented roof'. It is probably in part of it that the Exeter mint of Mary Arches Street (whose silver coins bore the letter E under the bust of William III) operated between 1696 and 1698. On this site is now the car park which spreads to a wasteland at the back of the North Street houses.

Opposite the car park, No. 18 Mary Arches Street, an eighteenth-century brick building erected on the remaining red sandstone walls of an earlier one, was probably used as stables. The double doors give access to the delightful garden of St Olave's Rectory, whose pond, fed by a natural spring, and lawns, are surrounded by an attractive variety of fifteenth-, eighteenth- and early-nineteenth-century houses.

Next to No. 18 is the walled recess of an old

Above: *Lants Almshouses, which originally stood on the City Wall, were removed in 1959 in anticipation of a major road construction.*

Right: *Lants Almshouses detail.*

conduit. An inscription tells us that the water was brought here for public use at the sole expense of James Galsworthy in 1839. Seven years earlier, in the days of the cholera epidemic, Mary Arches Street had been a centre where the poor would be given soup, and where, at the 'Station House', they could obtain blankets, 'hot air baths' and any equipment or drugs that were available.

The only other feature of interest in Mary Arches Street is the narrow three-storey, gabled house of No. 22 which possibly dates from the seventeenth century. This house and No. 18 may eventually be demolished.

Once, on the site of the Mitre Hotel and close to Bartholomew Street East, stood the late-sixteenth-century almshouses that John Davy, three times Mayor of Exeter, founded for six poor people 'two married couples and two single persons men or women.' These houses appear to have been demolished in the mid-1930s.

Between North Street and the green of Bartholomew Yard, there were on both sides of Bartholomew Street East, neat little houses which formed a most attractive townscape. The early-eighteenth century cottages on the south side were built of two shades of brick, and the almshouses which had been erected on the city wall were very picturesque. Now only the old malt-house remains.

Richard Lant's almshouses had been built in 1763 and stood on the north side of Bartholomew Street close to the Crown and Sceptre Hotel, partly on the city wall; there are flowerbeds and a small lawn now

where the front of the houses used to be!

The Lant Almshouses were removed in 1959 in anticipation of an extraordinary city council project. In the 1950s and early 1960s, the council was keen on cutting a main road across Bartholomew Street East and the green of Bartholomew Yard as a link to the west. The project was later abandoned.

The width and barrenness of Mary Arches Street; the widening, demolition and reconstruction in Bartholomew Street East; and the desecration of the natural beauty of the hills between Barley Lane and Exwick by having covered them with a multitude of unimaginatively set habitations, all make it now difficult to believe that 20 years ago one could have written, 'Emerging from the shade of this narrow way into Bartholomew Street East on a fine afternoon, one suddenly finds oneself in a blaze of light, commanding from the city wall fine views of distant country hills to the west, and enjoying the nearby sight of the 200-year-old cottages quaintly perched on the wall itself.'

Sources
Express & Echo and *Western Morning News* reports (1950–54)
(Alexander Jenkins (1806), *History and Description of the City of Exeter*
Thomas Shapter (1849), *History of the Cholera in Exeter in 1832*
Devon Notes & Queries (*Exeter Churches*, Beatrix Cresswell, 1908–09)
Hogenberg map of 1587

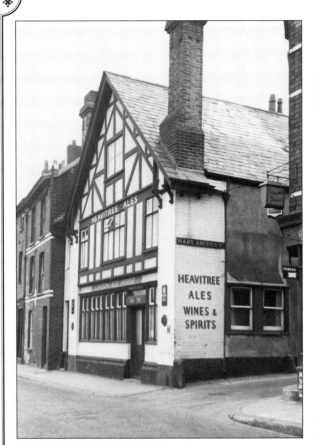

Left: *The original narrow entrance to Mary Arches Street from Bartholomew Street East.*

'Emerging from the shade of this narrow way into Bartholomew Street East on a fine afternoon, one suddenly finds oneself in a blaze of light, commanding from the City Wall fine views of distant country hills to the west, and enjoying the nearby sight of the 200-year-old cottages quaintly perched on the wall itself.'

(This, written in the 1950s, is no longer true).

Below: *Bartholomew Street East. Between the Old Malthouse and the Crown and Sceptre Hotel stood the eighteenth-century Lants Almshouses.*

✤ CHAPTER 14 ✤

The Bartholomew Street Area

When King Edward I, who was spending Christmas 1285 in Exeter, asked a member of his entourage where he was lodging, the Earl of Hereford replied that he was with the Franciscan monks 'in a horrible drain, where the place smells indoors and out', and that 'within two years nine brothers had died'. He added, 'Lord King, for God's sake, request the Bishop to provide them with a better place.'

This insanitary monastery, a friary, stood on the site of the green known since 1637 as Bartholomew's Burial Yard, which is now a public garden.

The condition of the whole area, although not as offensive as that of the Franciscan convent in the thirteenth century, is now one of appalling decay, due mostly to indecision and official neglect. Only a few years ago, this green with the eighteenth- and nineteenth-century houses of Bartholomew Street on two sides, the slopes of the Longbrook Valley, the heights of Mount Dinham, and the distant hills of Exwick on another, formed one of the most attractive parts of Exeter.

Historically, the site must be one of the most interesting in the West Country. According to one historian it is probable that the earliest inhabitants of Exeter lived in this area which is topographically, the top of a spur overlooking the River Exe.

Here these ancient Britons would have had an earthwork, and the name Little Britayne, which preceded that of Bartholomew until the seventeenth century, would have been a reference to those early days of the Celtic tribe of the Dumnonii.

The Romans, who founded Exeter (Isca Dumnoniorum) in the first century, erected an earth

Georgian houses facing the green of Bartholomew Yard. The buildings are shown in poor condition, with boarded windows in the end houses.

The Catacombs, built in 1835 as a burial place against a section of the City Wall.

The interior of the Catacombs.　　　　(J.W.)

bank around it in the second half of the second, and consolidated this rampart with stones in the late second century and early third. Here, on the north-western and south-western sides of Bartholomew Yard, the Roman wall followed natural defences, and one is aware of this today when walking on the footpath above the city wall and looking down towards Exe Street and the river at the bottom of the hill.

Another theory as to the origin of the name Little Britayne is that after the Saxon invasion and occupation of Exeter in the mid-seventh century, the Britons were segregated within this area of the town.

Mendicant monks of the Franciscan order settled in Exeter towards the middle of the thirteenth century and their first home was the site of Bartholomew Yard, hence the name of the narrow lane Friernhay Street, which once led from the principal street (Fore Street) to the Friary. In a petition of the time of Edward I, the friars were asking to be allowed to add to their property part of the highway towards the south and the east, 'leaving to the use of the King and citizens sufficient way for the passage of carts, which would be enough there, as men rarely pass by that way on account of the stench there, for there is in the said area a cesspool of the whole neighbouring street and the space between the said way and the church of the friars is only five feet.' By the early-fourteenth century the Franciscans were able to move to what was a better site then, about a mile away. That district is still known today as The Friars.

Documents in the city archives show that by 1514 the Prior of St Nicholas Priory and the city were quarrelling over the ownership of the old Franciscan site, both contending that they were entitled to it. A legal arbitration decided in favour of the city which had, however, to grant the Prior and his successors an annuity of 14s. These documents show in their precise descriptions how the king's highway there joined the North Gate to the West Gate (within the city wall). We therefore know that this street pattern still exists, although the road is now wider.

By the 1580s the old site of the Franciscan convent was used as a rackfield. This is where cloth was dried on tenters – also called racks – after being treated in the nearby fulling mills. Those were the days of Exeter's woollen trade.

Then again, in the seventeenth century, the function of this site changed. Until then, the main burial ground for Exeter had been the Cathedral Yard, but by that time, 'the accumulation of corpses and mounds of earth threatened to bury the very cathedral.' So an eloquent appeal to the Corporation by the Bishop of Exeter, Joseph Hall, resulted in the city chamber giving the old monastic site to be used as the city's new burial ground.

Being consecrated by the Bishop on 24 August 1637, St. Bartholomew's Day, the site acquired the name of St. Bartholomew's Burial Yard, and the street which adjoins it changed its name to Bartholomew Street. A wall erected on two sides, and the ancient city wall, formed the enclosure. Later, houses were built on its south-western (river) side.

The Lower Cemetery, nearby, on the steep slope between the city wall and Exe Street, was consecrated by Bishop Phillpots on 24August 24 1837, exactly 200 years after the consecration of Bartholomew's Yard. Some 30 years ago, both cemeteries were turned into public gardens. A curious feature of the Lower Cemetery is its catacombs, built in 1835 against a section of the city wall. They were hardly used for burials, but the 20 arches, on both sides of the long

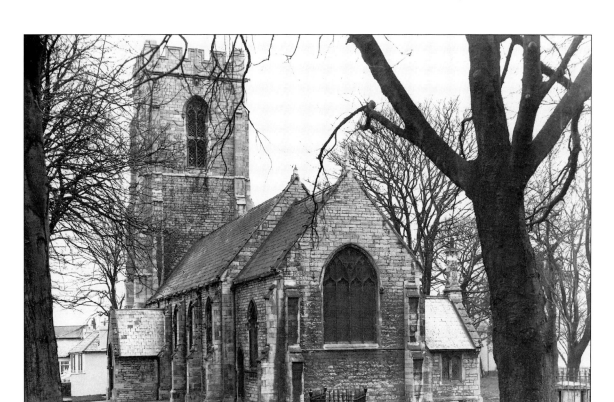

Allhallows Church, Bartholomew Yard, built in the nineteenth century, replaced the original church which stood on the City Wall. The Victorian church was demolished after the last war.

The font of Allhallows Church now in a courtyard off Bartholomew Yard.

gallery, were given light through narrow apertures all along its length. This interesting and unusual structure (for this country) is now in a bad state of decay.

A church was built at the south-western end of Bartholomew's Yard in the mid-nineteenh century and was named Allhallows-on-the-Wall to recall the medieval church of that name which had been demolished in the 1770s, with a section of the city wall on which it stood, when New Bridge Street was made. The Victorian church was demolished some 30 years ago.

On the land between Bartholomew Street and Fore Street, used to stand seventeenth- and eighteenth century houses of great charm if not of great architecture. They could have been modernised and restored before they became too decayed for renovation; instead, within the last 20 years, they have been demolished. However, Friernhay Street has retained its shape since the thirteenth century. As well as leading to the Franciscan Friary, it was the south-western boundary of the Benedictine Priory of St. Nicholas whose cemetery was on this side. Since the ancient street-pattern of Exeter, which had remained unchanged for centuries, although new buildings were erected from time to time, has been much disturbed in the reconstruction of the city after the last war, it would be a good thing to keep Friernhay Street intact in width and shape when the area is redeveloped.

Looking at the sorry state today (July 1978) of the Georgian houses in Bartholomew Street, it does not seem possible that only a few years ago one could have referred to them as 'dazzling'. Let us hope that these listed buildings will be restored rather than demolished.

Sources
A.G. Little and R.C. Easterling (1927), *The Franciscans and Dominicans of Exeter*
Deeds relating to St. Nicholas Priory and to the site of Bartholomew Yard (Record Office)
W.G. Hoskins (1960), *Two Thousand Years in Exeter*
Maps of Exeter from 1587 to 1860.

Aerial view of the Friars area pre-war.

Magnolia House, early-eighteenth century.

Colleton Villa.

CHAPTER 15

The Friars

The Grey Friars, monks of the Franciscan Order, first settled in Exeter in the second quarter of the 13th century, on a site wrlich some 400 years later became known as Bartholomew's Burial Yard. As we have seen, it was a most unsatisfactory part of the city at the time, but it was not without difficulty that the Friars found a more suitable site to build on.

Although the Bishop of Exeter, Peter Quivil, had promised King Edward I to provide the Friars with a better place, and Quivil actually allowed the Franciscans to 'seek within and without the city a place where they might conveniently dwell', when they did find one the Bishop, influenced by his own priest ('they have come into the centre of your barony'), changed his mind.

At a banquet, on 30 September 1291, on being asked why he had not fulfilled his promise to the king, the Bishop replied, '[do you] wish to drive me out of my bishopric? By St. Peter, I will be strangled on the day they enter the place.'

That the next day, 1 October, Bishop Quivil actually choked while drinking some syrup and died, probably helped the Friars to bring their negotiations for the new site to a conclusion! The Franciscans eventually acquired over six acres of land and the building of the new friary began in 1303.

This site gave the name The Friars to a whole district of Exeter, which is bounded by Melbourne Street, Colleton Crescent, Friars Gate and Holloway Street, and which includes Melbourne Place and Friars Walk.

Brothers of this Franciscan mendicant order, like the Dominicans, were very proficient in theology, highly educated, and were in the thirteenth century the learned members of recently founded colleges at Oxford, but they had to live in poverty and work or beg for their subsistence. However, some of the Friars at Exeter must have fallen short of this high standard, for it is recorded that in 1419, prompted by the lay authorities' promise, Nicholas the Sergeant and Dick the Porter handed over prisoners who had taken refuge at the friary. The monastery received from the city two gallons of wine and 42s. worth of beef and mutton as a reward for its co-operation!

Magnolia House and Lawn House, in Friars Gate, (once one house, and built in the early part of the eighteenth century) are on the site of some of the original monastic buildings. Two massive doors in Magnolia House, one with peep-holes filled in and painted over; the other with a grille plastered over and also covered with paint now, could have belonged to the friary and been incorporated into the later building. Then, when Lawn House underwent some repairs in the mid-1950s, steps were discovered under the ground floor, which were believed to go to a passage once giving access to the river. The garden's retaining wall extends to Quay Lane and before the thoughtless reconstruction of that narrow way a few years ago, from it could be seen traces of the friary's back gate in the fifteenth-century red sandstone wall.

When the attractive Regency style houses of Friars Walk were built in 1833, human bones were excavated, and 2ft below the ground was found a stone whose translated Latin inscription is, 'Here lies

Colleton Crescent, erected between 1802 and 1814 by Exeter builder Nosworthy.

Melbourne Street before restoration.

Terrace of early-Victorian houses in Melbourne Place, all demolished.

Victorian houses of Melbourne Place being demolished.

Detail of windows.

Brother Roger Davnat Doctor in holy theology who died on the 12 December 1516.' After the Dissolution of the Monasteries, the property of the Grey Friars was let on lease to John Hull of Larkbeare (remains of that fifteenth century mansion form part of the Elizabethan Service Station in Holloway Street), and eventually the eminent Exeter merchants, the Colletons, acquired the site.

When John Colleton returned from Barbados at the Restoration of the monarchy, Charles II gave him the rank of Baronet and some land in Carolina. It was his grandson, also John Colleton, who brought into this country from Carolina the first magnolia. He settled in Exmouth but kept the Exeter property of his ancestors, and it is possible that the magnolias of Magnolia House derive through cuttings from the original shrub brought to Exmouth. The site of the old friary with its grounds remained in the hands of the Colletons until the early-nineteenth century, when it began to be developed.

The nine brick houses of Colleton Crescent were erected by the Exeter builder Nosworthy between 1802 and 1814. These houses have round-headed

doorways with decorated keystones of Coade stone representing faces, and, following Georgian fashion, their elegant windows are of decreasing height with each higher floor.

Colleton Villa, which we face as we go down Friars Gate from Holloway Street, was built in about 1820. It is a house of excellent proportions in the classical style of the period, with a wide pediment below the roof line, and a small one, supported by two Ionic columns, which forms the porch of the entrance.

By the middle of the nineteenth century Friars Walk, Melbourne Place, and Melbourne Street had been built, and until the late 1960s the whole area in spite of some neglect here and there, and the need for restoration, had still much that was attractive. The slope and curves of the narrow streets converging to form a little square, the proportions and beautiful bricks of the Georgian crescent, the charm of the small early-Victorian houses, the clean sweep of the Regency ones, the gardens with their graceful trees and colourful stone walls, all formed a delightful townscape which well deserved the city council's decision in 1968 to designate The Friars as a Conservation Area. But a few years later, in anticipation of a vast road project which was later abandoned, the area was appallingly maimed.

Melbourne House, unique in Exeter, stood in its own garden whose surrounding red sandstone wall was an attractive feature in Friars Walk, Melbourne Place and Holloway Street. This eighteenth-century gabled house of fine proportions had a mansard roof like the hull of a ship and an elegant interior which included several unusual alcoves. There is nothing left of this building or of the surrounding colourful garden wall.

In Melbourne Place stood a handsome group of eight early-Victorian houses which formed a stuccoed terrace whose charm was enhanced by the last three houses being set back at an angle. Most of the windows had retained their original pediments and console brackets. The whole terrace was inexcusably demolished, and so were, between Melbourne Street

The junction of Friars Walk with Holloway Street. Melbourne House and most of the houses between the two streets were demolished.

Remains of fifteenth-century Larkbeare.

The eighteenth-century Melbourne House.   (J.W.)

The fifteenth-century ceiling of Larkbeare.

and Melbourne Place, ten unusual houses whose parapets were decorated with shell and flower ornaments and whose long front gardens reached Holloway Street.

This part of The Friars is now being redeveloped, but although what is being erected seems to be, so far, pleasant enough in shape, it does not excuse the destruction of the attractive nineteenth-century houses which stood on the site.

Fronting Holloway Street, the new buildings form an unusual façade in zigzag shape, like so many bows of ships. On the Melbourne Place side, the protruding part of the houses – where the entrance doors are placed – forms recesses where are pairs of windows. This is visually interesting, and so are a pleasingly eaved gable, and the slant facing Friars Walk, which is created by the uneven outline of the buildings.

Sources:
Deeds relating to the site (Record Office
A.G. Little and R.C. Easterling (1927), *The Franciscans and Dominicans of Exeter*
Alexander Jenkins (1806), *History of the City of Exeter*
The author's own report on behalf of the Civic Society, for the city council, 1968

The South Gate reconstructed for Queen Victoria's Jubilee, 1897.

A drawing of the South Gate from outside the City Wall.

CHAPTER 16

The South Gate Area

One of the two most inhuman areas in Exeter is formed by a fairly large site where Holloway Street, South Street, Magdalen Street, and Western Way (the inner by-pass) bleakly meet in an appalling barrenness whose sole relief is that of street lamps and signposts. This has been achieved without the help of a wartime enemy, simply by creating Western Way where buildings used to be, and demolishing a considerable number of picturesque houses and courtyards along the three ancient streets, which, until the early 1960s, had met in happy neighbourliness and secure intimacy.

Magdalen Street takes its name from an ancient chapel and hospital dedicated to St Mary Magdalen, and probably founded in the twelfth century for those who had contracted leprosy after the disease had increased on the return of crusaders from the East. The buildings stood in Magdalen Street, above Bull Meadow, just beyond the site of Fairpark Road.

Wynard's Almshouses

Wynard's Almshouses fortunately remain with us. Their local red standstone, general outline, and

The exterior of Wynard's Almshouses, originally fifteenth century, rebuilt in 1675, restored in 1864.

Part of the courtyard of Wynard's Almshouses.

cusped, mullioned, two-light windows are typical of fifteenth-century Exeter. But the houses were considerably damaged during the Civil War, were rebuilt in 1675 and restored in 1864.

The cobbled inner court, with its ancient well and fine, dark-green holm-oak, is a peaceful, old-world retreat. The almshouses and their chapel were founded in 1436 by William Wynard who was Recorder of Exeter for some 25 years. The foundation was 'for the increase of God's worship and for the relief of infirm people who were unable to maintain themselves.' A resident chaplain was appointed, and 12 deserving poor people were carefully selected to reside there. By tradition mayors of the city had to visit the houses twice a year to hear complaints from the residents. On each occasion, a flagon of wine and ale were provided by the chaplain for the mayor and his retinue.

By 1951, the scheme was administered by the Exeter Municipal General Charities, but 20 years later, the city council restored and modernised the interiors of the houses, which were then adapted to a different use. They have since housed various voluntary social service organisations.

Palmer's Almshouses

A little further on in Magdalen Street, towards Southernhay, the small portion of an old wall, surmounted by a gable flanked by two plain ornaments, recalls that here stood, long ago, Palmer's Almshouses, 'presented as habitation for four poor women' by John Palmer in 1487. He was an Exeter

Palmer's Almshouses.

Old Magdalen Street before some of its buildings were demolished, c.1910.

The last resident of the Almshouses, Mr Clarence Elvin.

baker who left his property in trust for the benefit of his foundation: four houses with two rooms each and a garden, where poor widows chosen by the City Chamber could live.

Gabled Houses in Magdalen Street

On the other side of Magdalen Street, where cars clock-in and await their owners, the tarmacked site now spreads drearily between two roads, in front of the Acorn public house. Here stood until the 1960s a fascinating triangle of unevenly and attractively shaped houses, which extended to Holloway Street and ended with a seventeenth-century inn called the Valiant Soldier, at the angle then formed by Holloway Street and Magdalen Street.

Red Lion Court, Magdalen Street.

Among these, one of four Jacobean gabled houses in Magdalen Street had a courtyard which still retained its well although it was no longer in use when the houses were demolished.

Another of these houses had a cobbled passage to a court from which a flight of stone steps led to the front doors of two dwellings. This was Bowden's Place, and in its happy, simple design, it had incredible charm. Beyond the first court, and past a fine, early-nineteenth-century iron gate (now in the garden of St Nicholas Priory) was another little courtyard where a hefty sandstone buttress held the lower portion of a tall slate-hung house. The narrow cob-wall passage of one of the houses led to an alley from which could be seen the slightly sagging ridges of original slate roofs. Eventually, through this enchanting maze, one could reach Holloway Street.

Burial Grounds

At the corner of Bull Meadow Road and Magdalen Street is the old, badly neglected Unitarian burial ground, and a little further on, adjoining it but separated from it, can be seen the Jewish cemetery. On the other side of Magdalen Street was the eighteenth-century Quakers' Meeting House, with the cemetery at the back. This is where Doctor Michael Lee Dicker was buried in 1752. The Register of the Society of Friends records that he died after a 'tedious and lingering illness which he bore with uncommon patience and a perfect resignation to the will of God' and that 'he was a man of great endowments and of a very extensive understanding both in regard to natural, political, moral and divine subjects.'

Magdalen Street Houses

The greatest loss sustained in the area is that of a group of eighteenth- and early-nineteenth century houses in Magdalen Street, which were demolished in July 1977. Doctor Dicker's house was one of these. It was originally called Magdalen House, but later became Nos. 39/40 Magdalen Street. It had been

A row of seventeenth-century houses and the original Acorn Inn in Magdalen Street, now all demolished. (J.W.)

The old Acorn Inn.

Bowden Place, a courtyard in one of the seventeenth-century houses in Magdalen Street. (J.W.)

threatened with demolition in 1964, and again later until 1974, by various road projects. After that year it seemed safe, and it has never really been made clear why it was not properly looked after; why it was demolished instead of restored.

The façade of Magdalen House was remarkable. The dentil band and ovolo decoration of its pediment, the shells, acanthus leaves and urns of its frieze, which ran the whole width of the façade, made it unique in Exeter. Doctor Dicker probably built the house in 1727 when he married. He was a man of simple tastes who believed that a house should be adorned on the outside where it could be seen by all, he himself being satisfied with a plain

The junction of Holloway Street and Magdalen Street with the seventeenth-century inn The Valiant Soldier and other buildings, now demolished.

Breaching of the City Wall in the making of Western Way.

Nos 39–40 Magdalen Street, originally built by Dr Dicker, probably in 1727. Most of these houses were demolished in 1977.

James Street originally joined Coombe Street and South Street. Its houses could have been modernised and restored. All buildings were demolished.

interior. This made his contemporaries remark that the doctor's house was built inside out! Michael Lee Dicker was one of the original six physicians appointed to the staff of the new Devon and Exeter Hospital in 1741.

Later in the eighteenth century, Magdalen House was the home of John Milford, the wool merchant who, in 1810, was for the year Master of the Corporation of Weavers Fullers and Shearmen. His son John sold the house in 1868 and it was after this date that it was divided and that shops were eventually added.

In later years the building had suffered great neglect, but in the early 1960s it was still in reasonably good condition. It was possible to see, within its walls, both the early-Georgian features of the Dicker House and the late-Georgian alterations dating from John Milford's time. One could see from Trinity Street, at the back of the house, how shallow the original building had been.

In the passage leading from the front door to the staircase, were four fluted pilasters that may have had some connection with the original staircase, which would have been between the two ground-floor rooms (these became the shops later). The late-

The same junction today.

Georgian staircase, further in, with typical slender bannister and balusters, remained until the demolition of the building. It was lighted by a glass cupola within whose drum was an ornate garland typical of the Adam and Regency periods.

On three levels the house had arched doorways which linked the early building to its later addition. A door, and part of a panelling belonged to the original house, as did eight of the window openings in the front, although the two tall windows dated from the late-Georgian period.

Next to Magdalen House, and demolished at the

Quay Lane seen from Quay Hill as it was.

Quay Lane in 1979.

same time, was a terrace of Regency-style houses which curved elegantly round the corner into Southernhay. When it was being dismembered, in June 1977, the 300-year-old framework of an original building, with cob filling and brickwork, was discovered, and so were such important features as a massive beam with the date 1659 and the initials I.M. carved on it, a seventeenth-century panelling, a fine staircase with typical seventeenth-century ballusters, and two fireplaces of the same period. The work of demolition continued.

South Gate

A plaque fixed on a wall outside the dilapidated, disused Holy Trinity Church, in South Street, shows where the medieval South Gate stood. It was, with its prison, and the original Holy Trinity Church, demolished in 1819. The South Gate was one of the gates which, as openings in the city wall, gave access to the old city. Very close to the gate, and just within the city, was the Gothic Church of Holy Trinity. It appeared, at a distance, to be part of the gate. The tower of the church projected into the street and narrowed it considerably. The gate had a round arch on the city side, and a pointed arch on the other. It was a massive structure flanked by circular towers, and part of it was used as a prison for debtors as well as for criminals.

Roman Gate and City Wall

Opposite the present Church of Holy Trinity, on the side wall of a new shop, and facing a section of the city wall, there is a plaque that indicates the site of the Roman gate. Its foundations were discovered in 1964 in the course of excavations, and at the same time, the archaeologist, Lady Fox, also found two layers of Roman road, which ran between the gate, and part of the rampart that surrounded the city and preceded the stone wall which was begun by the Romans in the late-second century. The best remaining section of the city wall can be seen on the other side of the inner by-pass. Its volcanic stones, dark-purple in colour, and neatly cut, are the Roman ones. The whole width of the inner by-pass here corresponds to the stretch of wall which, with James Street, was demolished to make the new road.

Quay Lane

Western Way was pitilessly cut across a visually and historically interesting part of Exeter where three ancient streets met. On the south-west side of Holloway Street–South Street, its making destroyed part of an excellent section of the city wall, a considerable number of small houses which had as much character as the ones removed from Magdalen Street, and the original, historical shape of the very ancient Quay Lane. Long ago, it had been a busy thoroughfare, for all goods landed at the Quay had to be carried through it to the walled city.

Among the houses, one of the victims was No. 82 Holloway Street. It was an early-eighteenth-century house which had been altered towards the end of that century as was shown by the fluted pilasters of its entrance, the Greek temple ornaments of its frieze (metopes and triglyphs), the bow window of its first-floor, and the Adam fireplaces and alcoves of its interior.

The opening from Holloway Street into Quay

A local resident enjoying a walk up Quay Lane, 1936.

Lane was so narrow that it was easily missed, and its tiny houses partly concealed the city wall, but with its gradually acquired features, it had character, variety and charm. Traces, in an old stone wall, of a fifteenth-century doorway once the back entrance into the grounds of the Grey Friars, the top of the city wall (there its original 18ft high), the cellars, the tiny shop of the cabinet maker, the merging Horse Lane with its steep twists, cobbles, and stone steps, all these were part of the fascinating Quay Lane. Its name has been preserved in a wide, grass-lined, tidy pedestrian way, and the new Quay Lane still leads to the Quay!

Sources
Report of Charity Commissioners (Exeter), 1825
Past owner's deeds relating to Magdalen House
Deeds in Record Office relating to Magdalen House
Register of the Society of Friends
Society of Friends' monthly minutes
J. Delpratt Harris, *Royal Devon and Exeter Hospital*
J. Tallis's map of 1860
Express & Echo report on Roman excavations in South Street, 29 July 1964
Express & Echo report on architectural discoveries in a Magdalen Street house, 27 June 1977
A. Jenkins, *History of Exeter*

✦ CHAPTER 17 ✦

The College of the Vicars Choral and Bear Tower

The ruin at the top of South Street, near the bus stop, is what remains of the hall of the 'College of the Vicars Choral of the Choir of the Cathedral Church of St. Peter.' The hall, which had a lovely sixteenth-century interior, including a remarkable chimney-piece, was used until its destruction during an air raid in 1942. But at least its ruin, with some interesting architectural features, has been preserved. The other buildings, which were part of the College, and formed with the hall a fine and picturesque group, were completely demolished between 1850 and 1900.

The numerous daily services held in the cathedral required an adequate number of priests and singers, and Bishop Brantingham had, for the use of this body, the College of the Vicars Choral, a hall, kitchen, houses and other buildings erected in 1387. When this was completed, the Bishop requested the Dean and Chapter to see that the vicars did reside within the College and observe his statutes.

In Cromwell's days, the City Chamber used the hall as a 'common wool hall' – the wool market was nearby in South Street – but at the Restoration of the monarchy, the hall and other buildings were all returned to the College of the Vicars Choral.

Originally, there was no entrance into the College from South Street: an outer wall followed the line of the street. On the site of the sloping ground between the remaining archway and the pavement of South Street, was a passageway or 'screens' which divided the hall from the kitchen, buttery and pantry (site of the new shops). These buildings extended as far as Little Stile, a narrow passage which connected South Street with the Cathedral Yard and still existed before the postwar reconstruction of this area.

The lane past the remaining archway, at the back of the ruins, and leading to the cathedral, was called Kalendarhay. On either side of it were the vicars' houses and at the cathedral end of it was a gatehouse, which made it an enclosure.

When at the Restoration the College buildings were returned to the Vicars Choral, the kitchen was let. Converted into dwelling-houses, it was let throughout the seventeenth, eighteenth and nineteenth centuries. Eventually it became the Bear Inn, taking its name from the ancient inn which had once stood on the site of the church of the Sacred Heart at the corner of Bear Lane and South Street.

Deprived of its kitchen, the hall was not used again as a dining-room after the seventeenth century, but it remained a common room and a music room. Also from the seventeenth century, the vicars no longer resided in their houses of Kalendarhay which were then let. In 1850, 20 of these medieval houses were still standing, but eventually the ones on the south side were demolished, the site becoming part of the Deanery garden; later, the ones on the north side were pulled down to make room for the new church of St Mary Major; and finally the rest was removed in 1900. The gatehouse, with its muniment room above, was demolished in 1872.

The interior of the fourteenth-century hall, which had been altered in the first half of the sixteenth century, had a fine oak panelling and a magnificent stone fireplace, whose large, carved lintel represented the arms of several bishops of Exeter. Part of this lintel, with the arms of Bishops Brantingham, Lacy and Oldham, is still in existence, at St Nicholas Priory.

The gate-house in Kalendarhay.

Interior of the Vicars Choral showing the fireplace whose remains are at St Nicholas Priory.

South Street entrance to the College.

The College looking west. These houses were demol-ished when the Victorian Church of St Mary Major was erected. (From a drawing of 1889.)

Vicars College, bombed in 1942, photographed in the late 1970s.

Although the ancient Bear Inn was further down South Street, another inn of the same name was later housed in what had been the kitchen of the Vicars Choral. The picture shows this second Bear Inn being demolished in 1871. In the background is the Church of St Mary Major (erected in 1865–68, demolished in 1971). The railings in the foreground probably surround the churchyard of St George's Church, which was demolished in 1843.

The back of The Bear Inn during demolition. In contrast to later additions can be seen the stone and timber work of the Vicars Choral's medieval kitchen.

Bear Lane and the Tower Site in the early 1980s.

Bear Tower stood at the corner of South Street with Bear Street. (J.W.)

Bear Tower before demolition.

The hall remained in all its splendour until its destruction in the war. All that is left now are part of the four walls, two windows, a doorway, and two buttresses. The stones are of the purple, volcanic variety known locally as Pocombe stone. Each window, within its outer arch, has two cusped lights formed by one mullion and divided by a transome, and a quatrefoil ornament above. These fourteenth-century windows are typical of the Decorated period of Gothic architecture.

A little further down South Street, at the corner of Bear Lane, stood until January 1966 the substantial remains of a fourteenth-century building, which had acquired the popular name of Bear Tower. This building had been incorporated into a house in the nineteenth century, part of which served as a shop until the air raid of 1942. Afterwards, for 24 years, only the medieval ruin remained.

The lower part of a doorway in it, was higher than the level of Bear Lane. This is because in 1839 South Street, which had been steeper here, was lowered, together with the adjoining streets. Close to the ruin's remaining doorway was a square-headed narrow slit of a window and on the east wall could still be seen a large blocked archway. The stones that formed the building were volcanic. Volcanic stones were the kind mostly used in Exeter since Roman times and until the sandstone quarries at Heavitree began to be used extensively in the fifteenth century.

The preservation of this interesting ruin had been considered, but in December 1965, the City Council obtained permission from the Minister of Public Building and Works to demolish it, 'subject to the foundations being preserved and laid out in a garden on the site.' Instead, a plaque has been inserted in a new paving, beneath which, quite concealed, lie the foundations of Bear Tower!

Sources:
Elijah Chick, *The Hall of the Vicars Choral*
J. F. Chanter, *The Customs and College of the Vicars Choral of the Choir of the Cathedral Church of St. Peter*
Devon and Cornwall Notes and Queries (A.W. Everett)
James Crocker (1886), *Sketches of Old Exeter*

✦ CHAPTER 18 ✦

The Globe Hotel

One of the casualties of the air raid of May 1942 was the Globe Hotel, which had existed on the same site, first as the Globe Tavern, for about 270 years.

It stood in the Cathedral Yard, facing the west front of the cathedral, where the backs of the new South Street buildings, and the pedestrian way to South Street are today. One end of the Globe Hotel's front was at right-angles with, and close to the southeast window of St Petrock's Church. Between the other end of the hotel, and the gabled houses which have survived, there was a footpath leading from the Cathedral Yard to South Street, called Little Stile; but there was also a pedestrian right of way through the hotel premises.

The hotel, at the time of its destruction, comprised two buildings of different styles: a four-storey Georgian one, and a three-storey building with dormer windows whose front obviously had undergone various alterations, but which was older.

When the Globe Hotel was advertised for sale in 1929, it was described as having 'finely carved doors and beautiful old panelling'. Actually, it was an engineer called George William Bannister (he was fascinated by Exeter's antiquities) who, seven years earlier, had discovered the original, complete, oak panelling in one of the hotel rooms. But in 1946, in *Music in Devon*, a paper he read for the Transactions of the Devonshire Association, R. Waterfield made a very intriguing statement: 'There is one more organ of the 17th century worth a reference, that existing at the Globe Inn, Exeter, in 1697.'

It has not been possible to establish precisely in what year the Globe Tavern began its life, but it appears that in 1648 the site was a garden whose owner was Elizabeth Crossing, yet, 26 years later the tavern was in existence. This is proved by the Parish Register of St Martin's which records the baptism 'on 25 October 1674 of Thomas, son of William Fowler, tapster at The Globe.' Apparently, however, the building was at first a private house, because in his will of 1711, Thomas Northmore left to his daughter Anna, the house in which he had 'formerly lived', but 'now divided into 2 tenements, one of which is the Globe Tavern.'

So it is reasonable to suppose that some time during the third quarter of the seventeenth century, the building was erected for the private use of the Northmore family. Thomas Northmore, who died in 1713, had bought in 1705, Cleve House at Exwick, and probably also the now-famous, so-called Tudor House, for both properties belonged to the Gubbs family and the Northmores owned them after the death of John Gubbs.

The name 'The Globe' given to a number of inns in the late-seventeenth and early-eighteenth centuries, probably has its origin in the trade which existed then between this country and Portugal, and whose importance was confirmed in 1703 by the Methuen Treaty that dealt with the exchange of port wine for English woollens. The globe or sphere, as the Portuguese Royal emblem, incorporated in the flag, derived from the armillary sphere: the arms of the House of Braganza which provided the kings of Portugal from 1640 until the republic was established in 1910. An armillary sphere is a skeleton celestial globe made up of hoops to show the motions of the heavenly bodies. It seems a reasonable assumption

The Globe Hotel and the south-east window of St Petrock's Church facing the green of the Cathedral yard.

Interior of the Globe Hotel.

Pre-war view of the Cathedral yard showing the Globe Hotel and the City Bank (later National Westminster Bank). Also shown is the spire of the Victorian Church of St Mary Major (demolished).

The blitzed Globe Hotel, 1942.

that inns which sold Portuguese wine should have adopted as a sign a stylised version of this sphere.

A detailed assessment among Exeter records, made in 1689-90, shows the relative importance of The Globe as a city inn. The New Inn had the highest rent or annual value of £196; the Signe of the Shipp the lowest at £6; while £65 was paid for the Globe Tavern by Thomas Robinson who ran it.

A plan of the tavern and adjoining buildings was drawn in 1772 by John Tothill, a surveyor, when

William Rigg, a maltster, took a lease of the inn, and two years later, a connection with Freemasonry was established when the Provincial Grand Lodge of Devon was founded there and Charles Warwick Bampfylde became its first Grand Master.

Also took place in one of the rooms of the Globe Tavern, the formation of a beekeeping society in 1797. This Apiarian Society met twice a year, but it only lasted a little over a decade.

In the summer of 1831, an advertisement appeared in the *Exeter and Plymouth Gazette* which announced that on 8 September a dinner would be held at The Globe to celebrate the coronation of King William IV and Queen Adelaide. Tickets cost 12s. each and the meal, which would include 'dinner, dessert, and a bottle of wine', would be served at 3 o'clock in the afternoon.

In the mid-nineteenth century, as well as being used during the training of the First Devon Militia as an officers' mess, The Globe was advertised as a family and commercial hotel, and in 1870, it was announced that 'to commercial gentlemen, families, tourists, and the public generally, this hotel will be found replete with every accommodation to ensure universal comfort.' It must have been appreciated too that there was always a night porter in attendance at The Globe, and that omnibuses called 'to and from the railway stations'.

The South-Street structures whose backs in the Cathedral Yard replace the front of the old hotel, unfortunately create a visual effect which is considerably inferior to that of the original buildings.

Sources
E. Lega Weekes (1915), *Topography of Exeter Close*
Re: earliest reference to The Globe (Devon & Cornwall Notes & Queries, entry from H. Tapley Soper, 1929)
Re: assessment of property for March 1689-90 (D & C N & Q, entry from W.G. Hoskins, 1939)
Will of Thomas Northmore (Record Office)
Obituary notice of George William Bannister (Transactions Of Devonshire Association, 1942)
Morris's Directory of Devonshire, 1870
Letter from City Librarian, June 1952
Exeter & Plymouth Gazette, August 1831
Express & Echo, May 1921
Devon and Exeter Gazette, December 1929

CHAPTER 19

The Bedford Street Site

On a plain wall of the General Post Office, a plaque dating from 1897 tells us that a Dominican convent occupied the site in 1259; that at the Dissolution of the Monasteries in 1539 it was granted to John Lord Russell, who converted it into Bedford House (where in 1644 was born Princess Henrietta, daughter of King Charles I); and that in 1773 the house was demolished and the construction of Bedford Circus begun. A smaller notice also tells us that the Victorian plaque was originally fixed to one of the Bedford Circus houses until they were destroyed by enemy action in 1942.

In his book *Exeter Phoenix, a Plan for Rebuilding*, Thomas Sharp's advice about Bedford Circus was to rebuild 'something of our own times which may be worthy of what went before', since it was 'so utterly destroyed that a man returning to Exeter and looking for it [could] walk over its site without knowing that he [was] doing so'.

But what Sharp does not appear to have realised is that after the air raid of May 1942, and before he came to Exeter with a view to preparing his project for the city (published in 1946), Exeter City Council had demolished the substantial remains of Bedford Circus. Although badly damaged, many of its lovely

The Bedford Circus plaque.

façades remained and the houses could have been rebuilt. To have destroyed it all is unforgiveable.

The site of the Dominicans' (Black Friars) monastery and grounds appears to have been approximately the area contained within Catherine Street, the service road almost in line with it (on the eastern side of Bedford Street), the present High Street Arcade towards Post Office Street, Post Office Street, and across Bedford Street to the service road behind the single-storey Bedford Street shops (Chapel Street). Since in 1232 King Henry III ordered the Constable of Exeter to allow the friars to get the stones they needed for the erection of their church from a quarry near the Castle, we know that this stone was the volcanic trap used in Exeter since Roman times – purple in colour and with small holes in it – which acquired the name of Northernhay stone. The church was consecrated in 1259.

Among the chief benefactors of the Friary were the Earls of Devon who were frequent visitors and had lodgings there. Communications between important citizens of Exeter and the Earls sometimes took place at this monastery. Hugh Courtenay was residing there at the time of his famous quarrel with the Mayor in 1306 over a 'kettle of fish'.

At the Dissolution of the Monasteries John Russell was granted the Friary and he converted some of the buildings into a town residence which, with Russell's title of Earl of Bedford, became known as Bedford House. There is no evidence that it had much architectural merit, but it was the administrative centre for the large Bedford estates in the Westcountry, and there, during the Civil War, Queen Henrietta Maria gave birth to her baby, Princess Henrietta Anne.

Bedford House being little used by its owners the Earls, and later the Dukes of Bedford, it was eventually converted into tenements which were let for many years to different tenants. Then it was demolished, the site and garden being let on a 61-year building lease by the Duchy of Bedford to Robert Stribling, an Exeter builder, and Giles Painter. There, Stribling erected Bedford Circus whose first stone was laid on 27 May 1773.

In the digging for the new foundations, a great number of human bones were discovered with the foundations of the Friary church. Among other relics, several lead coffins and a thick chest of lead (all containing human remains) were unearthed. 'All these were emptied of their contents for the small value of the lead, and the bones thrown among the rubbish, to the disgrace of humanity,' wrote an early-

Pre-war aerial view of the City, c.1930. Bedford Circus can clearly be seen in the centre of the photograph.

A section of Bedford Circus in prewar days.

nineteenth century historian.

Robert Stribling was born in 1727 and had been apprenticed as joiner to his father, also called Robert ,before he became a builder. From 1765 onwards he held the post of carpenter and joiner to Exeter Cathedral, but this seems to have been as a contractor, and while carrying out other works for his firm, Robert Stribling & Son. He appears to have lived in North Street.

According to his 'Description of the Manner of Building the houses of the Intended Circus at Exeter', the first stage was to build seven houses only – this on the eastern side. Fairly soon however, another seven were added on that side, but it was not until some 50 years later, in 1826, that the western side of Bedford Circus, which included the church, was

built.

The 'Description', after giving expected details relating to size, proportions, and materials to be used, has a section entitled 'Direction to Prevent Mischief Happening by Fire'. This is ironical if we consider that it was by fire that so much of Exeter was destroyed on that night of incendiary bombs in May 1942. But to prevent disaster by fire, Stribling had conceived for his Bedford Circus houses in 1773, a system whereby two girders in every other house would be laid from party wall to party wall, and two similar girders in the houses between would be laid from front to rear, while the roof timbers of each house would also be separated from those of the adjoining house by a fair space. No timber was to be placed too near flue or fireplace either.

High Street after its buildings had been severely damaged by enemy action and finally removed by demolition squads.

Façade and chapel of Bedford Circus after the air raid of 1942.

The aesthetic qualities of Bedford Circus were appreciated from the time its first houses were built until its substantial remains were completely removed by the local authority.

Robert Stribling was only a speculative builder, yet architects could justifiably write about his Bedford Circus houses, 'Not the least of the good qualities exhibited in this excellent grouping is the proportion of the windows and the subtle diminution in height between the storeys', and, 'The doorways are exceedingly well proportioned, and when viewed in perspective seem to check and steady the sweeping range of tiered windows.'

Bedford Circus was in fact probably the finest example we had of Georgian architecture in Exeter. The porches of the houses were particularly lovely with their simplified version of Corinthian columns. The single row of acanthus leaves came only halfway up the capital, and the upper part was fluted. The architrave above was also unusual, it consisted of three round ornaments separated by two bands of 15 short grooves. Above this was a dentil band and a plain frieze and cornice.

The festooned fanlights over the doorways were very fine, and the three sets of panels on the doors themselves followed the principle of diminution in height between the storeys of the buildings. It was this principle for the general line, the proportions,

and such details as those of the porches and doors which gave so much grace and elegance to these houses.

Early in 1951 the trees which had been in Bedford Circus were felled and removed, and the green at its centre became a dumping ground. A local observer remarked, 'The present indignities suffered by the green represent the last stage in the process of complete obliteration of the Circus as we knew it.'

On this site of the Dominican Monastery, which became the Bedford Estate, what have we today that has architectural merit? Could what is on the site of Bedford Circus be considered as 'something of our own times worthy of what was there before'?

Sources
A.G. Little and R.C. Easterling, *The Franciscans and Dominicans of Exeter*
Documents relating to Bedford Circus in the Record Office
A. Jenkins, *History and Description of the City of Exeter Exeter Flying Post* (Trewman's) 1780; *Express & Echo* 1951
A.E. Richardson and C.L. Gill, *Regional Architecture of the West*
Howard Colvin, *Biographical Dictionary of British Architects 1600–1840*
M. Rowe and A. Jackson, *Exeter Freemen*

✦ CHAPTER 20 ✦

Dix's Field

As we have seen in the last chapter, Thomas Sharp seems to have been unaware that much of Bedford Circus remained after the bombing of May 1942, and that it was the local authority which had demolished what was left. So he advised to rebuild on the site 'something of our own times'. However, the city council not having pulled down the houses of Dix's Field for some considerable time, Sharp was able to see the damage done to them by the air raid, and to recommend in his book *Exeter Phoenix, a Plan for Rebuilding* (published 1946), 'The walls of many of the smooth-fronted, finely-proportioned buildings still stand: they are gutted, smokeblackened, and their window voids gape open to the sky, but at least the shells remain. And moreover, some of the buildings stand unharmed... Restoration would be entirely justified.'

The city council decided to ignore this advice; to demolish nearly all these houses; and to replace them with the egg-box structure of the Civic Centre and a car park.

If we stand on the triangular pedestrian refuge which is in the middle of the road near the junction of Southernhay and present-day Dix's Field, we are on part of the site of what used to be No. 1 Dix's Field. This was erected by Matthew Nosworthy in the early nineteenth century, on land which had belonged to William Spicer Dix. It had been owned by his family for generations, hence the name Dix's Field.

This four-storey stuccoed house at the entrance of Dix's Field, with its bow windows, verandah, and criss-cross-patterned wrought-iron rail, was a typical 'Regency' house. It also had the distinction of being the place where the author, hymn-writer, and theologian, the Revd Sabine Baring-Gould was born in 1834.

Entrance to Dix's Field showing part of the Regency House, where the Revd Baring-Gould was born in 1834.

Residents of Dix's Field at the turn of the last century.

William Spicer Dix, like other members of his family before him, was in the woollen trade, and was Master of the Corporation of Weavers, Fullers and Shearmen in 1774. When he died at Sampford Peverell in September 1804, aged 68, the obituary notice in *Trewman's Exeter Flying Post* stated that he had been 'many years since a respectable merchant' in Exeter. As a businessman he had had his troubles, though, for in 1793 he was made bankrupt.

Dix, who had often been approached to grant building leases on his land called Dix's Field, was advertising in the *Flying Post* in January 1796 that he was willing to let or sell the whole or part of this land to build on. He pointed out that its situation was 'high, dry and healthy' and stated, 'springs of excellent water are found within a few feet of the surface.' But it seems that it was not until 1799 that Matthew Nosworthy acquired the property (after it had been in other hands following Dix's bankruptcy) and that it was some seven years later that Nosworthy began to build houses there as a speculation.

Matthew Nosworthy was born at Widecombe-in-the-Moor in 1750 but came to live in Exeter at an early age. He eventually acquired his own business as a builder in the city, and when he died at the age of 81, in 1831, the *Flying Post* recorded, 'All the handsome houses in the Barnfield and the Dix's Field were built by him; many of the houses on Southernhay and various other parts of Exeter also owe their existence to his persevering industry', and, 'He was unremittingly engaged in the extension of this, his adopted city and assisted to advance it more than any other individual by constructing mansions to invite the opulent to reside there.'

In May 1792, the same newspaper had been 'happy to inform our readers that the ground called the Barnfield... is contracted for by Mr Nosworthy, architect, for building a new crescent, consisting of at least 27 houses, which are to have... an extensive view of the country round.' The newspaper then added, 'This information must afford great pleasure to the gentry who frequent this city, as they will no longer be deprived of an accommodation, the want of which has so often occasioned complaint.'

Barnfield Crescent was still being built in 1806. Colleton Crescent, which it is assumed Nosworthy also built because its style is comparable to that of the other Georgian terraces he is known to have built in Exeter, had one of its houses advertised to be let or sold on the 20 September 1804 as 'a handsome new-built house'. By 1806 several of the houses of Colleton Crescent were occupied, and Southernhay was partly built. Nosworthy had also designed and erected the New London Inn in the early 1790s (present site of the ABC Bingo-hall).

Matthew Nosworthy began to build his Dix's Field houses after 1805, but a deed of 1818 specifies that he had 'lately erected divers dwelling houses and buildings on the same field and was then about to erect divers other dwellings and houses thereon' and another document gives us proof that by 1820 Nosworthy was still building houses on Dix's Field. An interesting point is that the occupiers of these houses had to share wells for their water supply, as well as the 'plantation, shrubbery, garden in front of the premises, and walks and paths in and out of them'

The Dix's Field houses, like all other Nosworthy

Pre-war Dix's Field looking towards Southernhay.

Dix's Field site in the early 1980s. The Civic Centre (left) *replaces the Georgian houses about which Thomas Sharpe wrote in 1946 'Restoration would be entirely justified'.*

Barnfield Crescent built by Matthew Nosworthy in the late-eighteenth and early-nineteenth centuries.

buildings, had elegance, and their architectural merit was recognised from the time they were built and the site between the north and south terraces was landscaped. Their balconies, with wrought-iron rails, were a pleasing feature; their brickwork contrasted happily with their stone dressings; and the balusters, grouped in panels over the upper windows of some of the houses, gracefully increased their vertical effect.

Incredibly, at the south-east end of Dix's Field, three of Nosworthy's houses were spared, but they are neglected and one wonders whether they will ever be restored or are simply awaiting an ignominious end, a fate that befell other buildings worth preserving in Exeter. What contributes to their pleasing effect is the proportion of their windows and the gracefulness of the fanlights of their doorways. The centre of the round-headed windows on the ground floor and the first floor windows are the same height, the lower sashes of the latter and the

upper sashes of the ground floor having all nine panes, while, also in reverse order, the lower and upper sashes of respectively the ground and first floors have only six panes. The second-floor windows are shorter than the others, each sash containing six panes.

To look at these still-fine houses, once part of Georgian Dix's Field, and then face the anonymous, bleached mass of the Civic Centre, which sprang up where the other Nosworthy houses used to be, is a very depressing experience.

Sources

Documents in Record Office relating to William Spicer Dix, Matthew Nosworthy and Dix's Field
H. Colvin, *A Biographical Dictionary of British Architects 1600–1840*
Trewman's Exeter Flying Post (1792-93, 1796, 1804, 1831)
A.E. Richardson and C.L. Gill, *Regional Architecture of the West of England*

The Higher Queen Street Market c.1935. Opened in July 1838, it closed as a Market September 1962

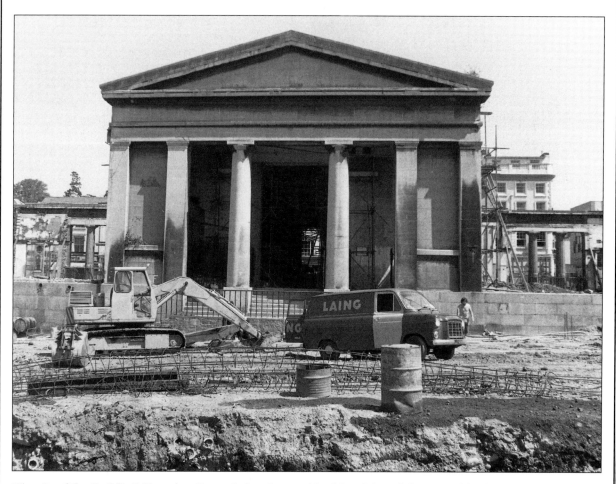

The site of the Guildhall Shopping Centre before the considerable raising of the ground level.   (J.W.)

✦ CHAPTER 21 ✦

The Higher Market
(or Queen Street Market)

It is commonly said that the architect of the Higher Market – usually called Queen Street Market since the destruction in the last war of the Lower Market – was Charles Fowler. But what is not generally realised is that originally the architect appointed for the Higher Market was George Dymond, and that most of it was actually designed by him.

This building, whose main body and attractive Queen Street façade mercifully remain with us, very narrowly escaped demolition after it had been closed as a market in the early 1960s.

The origin of this market – and of the Lower Market, which stood on the site of the present one in Fore Street – is the decision in 1833 of the Exeter City Chamber to make Queen Street, so as to join High Street to a new road (still called New North Road). Thus, Queen Street and its houses were built on a site where had stood other houses, inns, courtyards, and various open markets, in a maze of narrow streets and lanes. An Act of Parliament had to be obtained though (March 1834), before the city could get rid of its street markets and erect two covered ones instead.

The members of the City Chamber decided, so as to receive a variety of designs, that separate architects should be engaged to build the two covered markets.

Six prizes were offered: three for each market. The winner of the first prize in each case, would receive £100 and build the market according to his design, and the winners of the second and third prizes would receive £50 each. Naturally, the winners of the first prizes would also receive the usual fees for carrying out their work.

Charles Fowler won the first place with his design for the Lower Market; George Dymond the first place with his design for the Higher Market. But Dymond fell ill in August 1835 and died, at the age of 38, soon afterwards. At the time his market had been raised to little above the foundations. It was then that Fowler was appointed as the new architect, but he was requested to follow Dymond's plan. So apart from a few modifications, the Higher Market was mostly the result of Dymond's design. Certainly the Doric order and the general shape of the building were his, and although Fowler objected to the softness of Bathstone for the exposed parts, he was told he had to use it since it was already bought!

In contrast to Dymond, whose work was unknown (apart from some plans for a court of justice, drawn with another architect, and accepted by the Bristol Corporation) Fowler was already well-known in the country for work which included the Covent Garden Market in London.

The whole of the Queen Street façade of Dymond's Higher Market – beautifully cleaned – has been preserved. It comprises the four fluted columns and two pilasters of the main entrance, supporting the entablature over which is the pediment; and the two columns and pilasters supporting the entabla-

Goldsmith Street and rear view of Higher Market.

The well restored centre part of the Higher Market in the early 1980s.

The interior of the old Lower Market.

The Lower Market after the blitz (site of the Fore Street Market).

ture of the side entrances. By removing the shops that had been incorporated into the front of the building, space has been added to that of the porticoes, creating an attractive and convenient covered walk.

The central range of the old market has been retained and attractively restored. Its interior is formed by six square granite pillars on either side now also supporting upper-floor galleries. On both sides of what was the main hall of the market, there are now various shops where food stalls used to be. But what was the vegetable market, with a tie-beam roof supported by iron columns, and a light-giving clerestory, as well as the timber-roofed fish-market to the south of the remaining edifice, have all been pulled down.

The great disappointment though, is what has been done to the old market's main entrance in Goldsmith Street, which now forms part of a small square in the Guildhall centre. It was bad enough to demolish the sides, but it had been hoped that the original façade of this western entrance would be allowed to keep its excellent proportions. Unfortunately, the level of the ground in front of the building has been raised, thus removing not only the fine steps and iron railings of a platform which was an integral part of the façade, but also burying the next flight of steps, between the columns, and the whole deep base of these columns. There must now be a loss of at least 6ft in the elevation, so harm has been done, visually, to this classical façade by altering its carefully calculated proportions. Also, attaching it to new buildings, of no architectural merit, and whose shape, texture and colour scheme clash badly with those of the nineteenth-century façade, was a grave mistake.

The Higher Market had been opened on the 24 July 1838; it was closed for business on the 29 September 1962.

This text is based on the documents relating to the Higher Market in the city archives, and the *Biographical Dictionary of English Architects 1660–1840*

✦ CHAPTER 22 ✦

Gandy Street

A special study of Exeter's central area, produced in 1976 by the city council, refers to Gandy Street as a 'welcome, peaceful, backwater, tucked behind the High Street and Queen Street', whose narrowness 'reflects its origin as a mediaeval street'.

This is true of only part of this lane, for it was irretrievably maimed 20 years ago. Although the buildings which are on the site of the original ones are mostly Georgian and Victorian (there is a Queen Anne house at the corner of Gandy Street and Upper Paul Street), until the late 1950s it had remained a delightful and almost complete little street. Then, a section of its eastern side was swept away to accommodate the service road Musgrave Row opposite Little Queen Street. On the site of what is now a dismal gap, stood Nos. 30 and 31 Gandy Street.

No. 30 was a fine Queen Anne house scheduled as Grade II (it had been used for some time as the County Auction Mart). This house was set back from the street, having a forecourt of flagstones, once sur- rounded by iron railings. It had perhaps the best preserved Queen Anne doorway in Exeter. The porch hood was supported by typical carved brackets; the door had six panels; and the light above the doorway was composed of 12 small square panes of glass, also typical of the first quarter of the eighteenth century. The roof, below which was a coved cornice, was made of small grouted slates, and it seemed an added charm that its contour did not possess a straight line. Its interior had been altered, but original features, such as the shutters which folded neatly on either side of the window recesses, could still be seen in several rooms.

When the house was just over 100 years old, in 1828, it was occupied by Thomas Salter, a spirit and hop merchant who was also a maltster. The firm remained on the same premises for over 50 years, then another wine and spirit merchant took over. In the late-nineteenth and early-twentieth centuries a wine merchant was still there, but in this house was also the office of the surveyor Charles Ware; and before becoming the County Auction Mart in 1922 it had been used for some 15 years, until 1919, as the Soldiers' and Sailors' Institute.

The house next door, No. 31, was at the time of its demolition the Mitre Cafe, but until 1950 it had been for some 40 years the 'refreshment house' of the Streat family, where one could eat on the premises, or take away, delicious cooked meats. In 1910, William Streat had taken over the business from Mrs Emily Letheren who, four years earlier, had converted the dairy she had run since the mid-1890s into a refreshment house. The origin of the dairy had been Pengeley, a farm, from which had come John Wills who started Pengeley's Dairy in Gandy Street. In 1890, the premises were described as 'small but smart and bright in appearance', and 'irreproachably clean and sweet'. This was when the dairy had been awarded a prize at the Exeter Stock Show at the Lower Market (site of the present Fore Street market) for the quality of its milk products. 'The milk used for butter and cream or for daily sale by them, is of even a higher standard than what the average composition of cow's milk should reach.'

Before Goldsmith Street was practically destroyed in the 1970s, it was still possible to imagine the narrow lane at its Paul Street end, which had once joined it to Gandy Street (before Queen Street was made in the 1830s). Upper Paul Street is what remains of this link road, which continued across where Paul Street is today, to its junction with Goldsmith Street. This link between Goldsmith Street and Gandy Street appears as Corry Lane on the earliest map of Exeter, and what we call Gandy Street is shown as St Ian Cross, after an ancient cross whose precise site (close to what is the entrance to the forecourt of the old University College building) is still marked on early-eighteenth-century maps. By the last decade of the eighteenth century the name Corry, Carry, Curry or Carey had been replaced by Paul Street. As for 'Gandy's Lane', which in very early days also appears to have been called Correstrete (Corry Street), the name Gandy first appears in the early-eighteenth century. Although according to nineteenth-century sources this

Part of the shaft of this late-eighth-century Celtic cross (now at St Nicholas Priory) stood in Gandy Street, at the corner of High Street for nearly 150 years.

Queen Anne House (right) *at the corner of Gandy Street and Upper Paul Street.*

The Celtic cross at the corner of Gandy Street and High Street.

Gandy Street in 1979, showing its original width.

Little Queen Street, and beyond it, the new service road (Musgrave Row) where, until the late 1950s, stood Nos. 30 and 31 Gandy Street.

little street had been called St Lucie's Lane in the seventeenth century, this cannot be traced on maps or in documents.

The lane's name was changed in recognition of the importance of the Gandy family (Henry Gandy was Mayor in 1661 and 1672) who lived in this street. A document of 1658 shows that their house must have been near St Ian Cross, and another that the family owned the property until 1777. A John Gandy was Bailiff, Sheriff and Mayor at various times in the late-seventeenth and early-eighteenth centuries.

In about 1778, the market for fish, oats, grains and potatoes had been moved from High Street to a site between Goldsmith Street and Gandy Street, where part of the Swan Tavern had extended. To reach this new, colonaded, market place, on two sides of which were small shops and on another the Swan Tavern, a narrow way had been made from Gandy Street. This

allowed the passage of carts going to the market (a footpath existed from High Street). When all this was swept away in the making of Queen Street in the 1830s, the Carts' passageway became Little Queen Street, which to this day joins Queen Street to Gandy Street.

A little further on, there had been, for a considerable time, a narrow way leading from Gandy Street to Castle Street, when were erected, in the eighteenth century, the 'new buildings' which still give its name to the footpath now leading to the Rougemont Garden.

Near 'New Buildings', but on the other side of Gandy Street, is a passage to Queen Street. This dates from the erection in 1850 of a new Post Office in Queen Street. By the 1880s this building housed, on the first floor, the Episcopal Middle School for girls (Bishop Blackall), which was reached by an outside

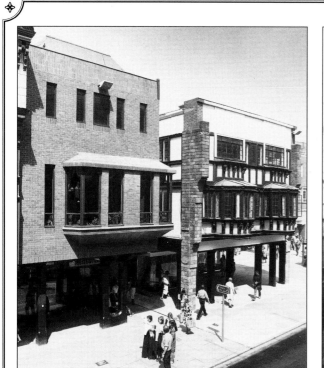

On the right No. 229 High Street as it has been since its reconstruction in the 1930s and with later alterations.

In 1930 the Jacobean interior of No. 229 High Street was removed and the house demolished. The photo, taken in the early 1930s, shows the new house with its copy of a seventeenth-century front. The upper bay windows and gables were replaced by modern features in the late 1930s.

The oak carvings of No. 229 High Street (corner of Gandy Street) were shipped to America in 1930 before this Jacobean house was demolished. The new building (incorporating a seventeenth-century bay window from North Street) became Lyon's premises.

The door of No. 229 High Street.

Queen Anne Porch of No. 30 Gandy Street.

The ceiling of No. 229 High Street.

iron staircase at the Gandy Street end of the passage. It can still be seen today in very neglected surroundings and itself in a decayed state.

At the corner of Gandy Street and High Street, an act of considerable vandalism took place in February 1930 when the Saxone Shoe Co. demolished a house which had stood there for centuries. This house, No. 229 High Street, had been for some 60 years the premises of the *Devon & Plymouth Gazette*, later the *Devon & Exeter Daily Gazette*, and a tobacconist had a shop there too. The shoe company erected a new structure on the site, and incongruously incorporated into its front, two bay windows, one of these having belonged to the long lost original façade of No. 19 North Street. Then, from 1933 and for some 40 years, Lyons occupied the new High Street building.

Before the house was demolished, the oak carvings of its magnificent Jacobean interior were ripped off the walls and shipped to America. The original façade though, had been replaced in the early-eighteenth century by one in the Queen Anne Style, which had four sash windows at first and second-floor levels and two in the attic.

This house, as a typical merchant's house, had considerable depth along Gandy Street. From the late-fourteenth century, when it was rebuilt with volcanic stones from the Thorverton area and red sandstone from Whipton, until the early-nineteenth century, it belonged to the Dean and Chapter of Exeter Cathedral and was leased over the years to many important citizens. Among others, John Shillingford, Receiver and five times Mayor, lived there until the mid-fifteenth century; Richard Duke, also Receiver and Mayor, occupied the house in the early-sixteenth century; and Thomas Bodley, founder of the Bodleian Library at Oxford, lived there as a child, and may even have been born in this house, for his father, John Bodley, took a lease of it in 1544.

It has been suggested that it was George Smyth, like the previous occupiers, a merchant, and also Mayor of Exeter, who rebuilt the interior of the house when he had it on lease from 1584, but the carved foliage and scrolls surrounding the wall panelling,

the figures dividing the oak panels over the chimney-pieces, and the columns, larger at the top than at the bottom, all had an exhuberance more consistent with the 1620s than the 1580s. There were also fine moulded plaster ceilings.

It seems likely that it was Roger Mallock (he took a lease of the house in 1627) who was responsible for the seventeenth-century alterations and adornment of the interior. After all, the house was known until its destruction as Mallock's House, and his arms were within one of the panels over a chimney-piece. Mallock, a wool merchant whose exports were considerable, was Mayor of Exeter in 1636. Between 1629 and 1646 he had made arrangements with the City Chamber so that his house could be used as the judges' lodgings.

When William Nation bought it from the Dean and Chapter in 1803, the house had been occupied by the Nation family for over 20 years. It was William Nation who had erected the shaft of the Celtic cross (now in the garden of St Nicholas Priory) at the corner of Gandy Street and High Street. He had acquired the stone when it was removed from the demolished Exe Bridge in 1778.

Gandy Street, although narrow, had become a very busy thoroughfare since the opening of the new market-place. Possibly it was the number of carts on their way there, which decided Nation to acquire this large stone so that with half its length sunk into the ground, it would become a firm and effective protection against wheels for the corner and wall of his house. The stone remained there for about 130 years (as can be seen, one side of the upper half of the shaft is very worn) and then it was for a while at the museum before being erected in 1916 at St Nicholas Priory where, according to one theory, it had been before being used to repair the bridge at the Dissolution.

In spite of the uninspiring blank walls which now oppressively flank this narrow lane at its High Street end, and the unfortunate gap created by Musgrave Row, this little street can still recall interesting fragments of Exeter's distant and fairly recent past.

Sources
Deeds relating to the Gandy family (Record Office)
Demolition of Ancient buildings of Exeter (Harbottle Reed, Transactions Devonshire Association, 1931)
Roger Mallock, Merchant and Royalist (W.B. Stephens, Transactions Devonshire Association, 1960)
The History of an Exeter Tenement (A.M. Erskine and D. Portman, Transactions Devonshire Association, 1960)
Maps of Hogenberg, 1587
Izacke, 1677
Sutton Nicholls, 1723
Charles Tozer, 1792
Besley's Directories 1828 to 1960
Where To Buy (a local Trades Guide, published 1890)

CHAPTER 23

Queen Street

Although a new street for the city was mentioned as early as June 1830 in the minutes of the Chamber, it was not until 1833, when New North Road was cut, that it was really decided to make the future Queen Street. New North Road begins at the top of Longbrook Street, by the ABC building, crosses the railway line and continues past the prison and the Clock Tower to join Cowley Bridge Road. As a convenient way from the north straight into the heart of the city, the future Queen Street was to join New North Road (at a point where, later, the Clock Tower was erected) to High Street.

The new street was partly the responsibility of the Turnpike Trust, partly that of the city, and it was developed from its conception to its completion over some 20 years. It was named Queen Street in 1838, the year of Queen Victoria's Coronation. Until then everyone had referred to it as 'the new street'.

We have seen in the chapter on Gandy Street that the High Street open markets had been moved in 1778 to a site between Coldsmith Street and Gandy Street, reached through Gandy Street itself and a

The opening in 1898 after the erection, the previous year, of the Clock Tower, at the junction of Queen Street and New North Road.

narrow way which later became Little Queen Street.

The intention, some 55 years later, had been at first that only parts of these markets would be removed in the making of Queen Street, 'for continuing the line of road into High Street, provided that the fish stalls be not interfered with and that no part of the Swan Tavern be encroached upon except the projecting part of the Great Room.' However, by 1841, that ancient inn was completely demolished; part of its site was incorporated into the new street; and the markets had vanished! This illustrates well what is still happening today: the difference between what is undertaken at the time of planning a project, and what has actually been done when the work is completed.

The final destruction of ancient features is very rarely proposed openly at first.

As we have seen in the chapter on the Higher Market, an Act of Parliament was obtained in March 1834 to enable the city to get rid of its street markets and to erect two covered ones; one of these became the Higher Market.

But if in the making of Queen Street, old inns, houses, courtyards and a maze of picturesque lanes were swept away, at least what was rebuilt on the site, in size, materials and shape, was not outrageously out of keeping with the adjoining High Street, even though it was in a different style. But if we now look at the C&A building at the corner of Queen Street and High Street, although we may find its height and brick acceptable, we are struck by the appalling unsuitability of such a structure for this site.

The length of its horizontal, monotonous roof line, and its dull, slitted but windowless walls, are a visual insult to all the older buildings nearby whose variety of roofs and façades forms a very pleasing geometry. The C&A structure owes its design to the combined efforts of that firm's architects, and of those officers who were the city council's Architect and Planning officials at the time. It owes its existence in that shape to the leniency of the Department of the Environment, and the passivity of the Royal Fine Art Commission and of the Exeter Civic Society. They were all approached by objectors of the design proposed for the site. They all gave weak reasons as to why they could not even try to stop the erection of such elevations.

On this site stood the premises of Boots the chemists until, in 1958, the firm moved to its new building at the top of High Street. But the old prem-

Queen Street. The corner with Little Queen Street and part of the original building (c.1850) which extended to High Street, can be seen on the right. This was later replaced by the C&A building.

The grand façade of the 1850 Post Office, and at the far end of the street, the C&A structure which replaces the nineteenth-century building.

ises became for a while John Webber's sports shop before being demolished some ten years ago.

These business premises had been part of a very attractive group of houses which extended into High Street from Little Queen Street and looked as if they were one building. The windows were of a decreasing height from the first to the third floor. They all had wide frames and were surmounted by small pediments on the first floor, and plain cornices on the second. At the top of the building was a cornice supported by corbels, and there were plain pilasters between some of the windows. It was an elegant façade with excellent proportions, which could have been restored and preserved.

When, in the making of Queen Street, this site was sold by the city in 1845 to the Revd Nathaniel Cole, the council specified that it would have to approve the elevation of the building erected there, as well as the line along which the foundations would be raised, and the shape of the corners (at the junctions Little Queen Street–Queen Street, and Queen Street–High Street, the buildings, including the windows, formed graceful curves very skilfully executed). Other conditions concerning Nathaniel Cole's property, were that the new buildings would have to be completed by 1849 and that meat, fish, poultry, butter, game, fruit, vegetables, cheese, or bacon would not be sold in any part of them. The fine if this condition was ignored, would be £1 per day of disobedience.

This clause was strictly adhered to over the years, and from the mid-nineteenth century the shop on the Queen Street side was occupied by a succession of stationers–booksellers, and that on the High Street side by dispensing chemists. In the 1880s and '90s here was the shop of Henry Will Harris, pharmaceutical and analytical chemist. Then, for about 30 years, until 1927, both sides became the premises of A. Wheaton the general stationers. The following year, Boots the chemists moved in, and they were also to occupy both sides for 30 years.

By 1835 Queen Street had been made to go through Paul Street (its north-east side becoming Upper Paul Street), through the city wall, and the garden walk of Northernhay. The wall and the walk had been continuous until Queen Street was cut, thus separating Northernhay Row (which became Northernhay Street) from Northernhay Garden. But in 1837 the approaches to the new market were still inadequate and it was feared that shoppers would find themselves 'mixed up in the most dangerous manner with waggons, carts and every description of vehicles.'

At the corner of Queen Street and Paul Street, next to the old market, (where now, a new structure has an unbecoming roof which looks like a heavy helmet) there used to be a fascinating building where generations of wine merchants had carried on their trade. It had been 'purpose-built'. The very high windows were round-headed and between them were pilasters which each ended with a finial above the roof line. The site was first let by the city to Thomas Sercombe in 1851. He was the first wine merchant to occupy the place and it was probably he who built the premises. Later, Benjamin Faville Carr carried on his business here, and from the 1870s until 1961 the premises were occupied by Carr & Quick the wine and spirit merchants, brewers, and at some time cider makers. Before this fine Victorian building was unnecessarily demolished in the early 1970s, it had been used for a few years by Holme Farm Dairy.

On the other side of Queen Street, at the corner it forms with Upper Paul Street, is a Georgian house.

In the centre of the photo can be seen the nineteenth-century building which extended from Little Queen Street to High Street.

Here in the 1870s and early '80s were the premises of Harding, Richards & Thomas, wine and spirit merchants. Their counting house was on the Upper Paul Street side; their stores fronted Queen Street. Then, by the late 1880s, the firm (which remained there until 1966) had become St Anne's Well Brewery, also wine and spirit merchants.

Next to it, in Queen Street, is an interesting group of three houses (Queen Street Chambers) divided by pilasters up to their eaves. The first-floor windows are surmounted by architraves supported by two brackets: a very pleasing group.

A little further on towards High Street, we come to the grand façade of the General Post Office which opened in 1850. The building was used as such for only 14 years. This edifice was erected by the Paris Street builders W.H. & W.W. Hooper. Its ornate classical façade, with its impressive Corinthian columns and cornices, contrasts with the sobriety of the rest of Queen Street, and with the simplicity of the Doric order of the old market across the street.

The four huge columns of this first Queen Street Post Office rest on a plinth at first-floor level, and their capitals reach the top of the second-floor windows. There is a large doorway between spacious windows in the rusticated front of the ground floor, and the round-headed, very high first-floor windows are surmounted by architraves supported by three brackets each. The second-floor windows are surrounded by a heavy square frame. Above, are a decorated corbel-table and a balustrade. This façade has recently been beautifully redecorated.

By 1864, the building had become too small to accommodate the General Post Office, which was moved to new premises, further away in Queen Street, next to the Northernhay Garden entrance. It remained there until its move to High Street in 1885. By that time, the grand Queen Street building housed on one side of its ground floor the Society for Promoting Christian Knowledge; on the other, a brewer; and above the ground floor, reached by an outside staircase, the Episcopal Middle School for Girls (Bishop Blackall), whose headmistress was Miss Mary Pemberton.

Between this building and the Queen's Hotel – whose façade has been preserved, and very well restored and redecorated – is a terrace of seven houses divided by pilasters which end, each, with a honeysuckle ornament level with the corbels below the cornice of the roof: an interesting and attractive façade. Then, from Little Queen Street to High Street, in graceless contrast, we now have the pile of the C&A structure.

Queen Street Corner.

The C&A building which replaced it.

This fine building, erected in 1851, formed the corner of Queen Street with Paul Street. It was demolished in the early 1970s and was replaced by the new structure.

The Carr & Quick site, 1979.

On the right, a Georgian house forming the corner of Upper Paul Street with Queen Street (the premises of Wine Merchants in the nineteenth century and until 1966). Further on, the Royal Albert Memorial Museum, and beyond it, the 1864 General Post Office.

The statue of Queen Victoria which dominated the building of George Ferris.

These well-known ornaments adorned the buildings erected by George Ferris in 1842 next to the market, later the site of Marks & Spencer.

This was the General Post Office from 1864 until the 1880s.

Much of the western side of Queen Street, between Paul Street and High Street, is occupied by the very handsome and well-restored façade of the old market which is the subject of another chapter. But next to the market, stood a fine group of houses which a large statue of Queen Victoria dominated. They have recently been demolished in the course of a Marks & Spencer site development. (The firm stated that the statue would be replaced with a copy of the original, and that it would stand on their new building.) The houses, which have been pulled down, and their owner, were praised with these words in 1848, 'George Ferris's name will remain in connection with the splendid row of buildings in Queen Street which he has the gratification of calling his own... Long may George Ferris live to enjoy the property which by thrift and perseverance and honourable industry he has accumulated.' The architect of these houses was Henry Lloyd and his plan had been submitted to the city council by Ferris in 1842.

The statue of the Queen was the gift of George Ferris who had it installed at his own expense on the day of Queen Victoria's birthday in 1848. *Trewman's Exeter Flying Post* reported, 'This morning the neighbourhood of Queen Street was all life and gaiety and animation. At an early hour, the statue was raised to the summit of the houses and safely secured upon the pedestal which had previously been prepared for its reception.'

The 130-year-old statue and buildings could have, no doubt, lasted many more years.

Sources
Documents in city records (Chamber and Council minutes and deeds relating to property) dealing with the making of Queen Street.
City Directories: 1853–1965
Trewman's Exeter Flying Post, May 1848
Maps of Exeter (J. Britton, 1805; R. Colliver, 1835; J. Tallis, 1860)

The corner formed by High Street and the western side of Goldsmith Street. This building, the premises of Knapman from the mid-nineteenth century until 1949, and later of Horne Bros, was demolished in 1979.

The north-west part of Goldsmith Street as viewed from Paul Street. Most of this street was swept away in the construction of the Guildhall Centre.

✦ CHAPTER 24 ✦

Goldsmith Street with the Churches of Allhallows and St Paul

Goldsmith Street, of medieval origin, had been so maimed in the erection of the Guildhall Centre, that it had become a mere stump linking High Street to a pedestrian square. Now that Marks & Spencer have demolished all the buildings, on the north-eastern side, of what remained of that street, between High Street and the square, and Horne have pulled down their own premises, on the south-western side, even the stump has nearly disappeared. What is left is simply an opening, a space, at the time of writing.

Although most of its buildings dated from the nineteenth century, the pattern of this narrow, ancient street had been very little altered until, in the early-1970s, two-thirds of its length was bulldozed out of existence, leaving only that part of it which is between the Waterbeer Street square and High Street. Before then, Goldsmith Street had joined High Street to Paul Street. Now, not only do the colossal structures of Paul Street, and other drab buildings of the new centre, stand on parts of its site, but where nothing has been erected over the course of Goldsmith Street, the level has been outrageously raised, as it has in front of the south-western entrance to the old market, thus completely spoiling the once-fine façade of this building.

Before the closure of the market in September 1962, that picturesque part of the little street was a centre of activity, but it remained fairly busy until 1965. By the following year, the shops had been closed, and that part of Goldsmith Street died. The last occupants (for another two years) were the Exeter Ambulance Service and St John Ambulance

The junction of Goldsmith Street and Paul Street, also demolished in the construction of the Guildhall Centre. The massive walls of the new structure replace the Paul Street Houses.

Brigade, who had been housed since 1949 in what had been until the previous year the Bull Hotel, whose last landlord was Robert Hamlin Dymond. This was No. 13 Goldsmith Street, a listed building, altered in the eighteenth century but obviously older, with an interesting early-Victorian glass and iron front at ground-floor level. All these quaint houses, some of them gabled, forming Nos. 5–14, were demolished, and their site became an extension of the temporary car park round St Pancras Church.

Goldsmith Street is mentioned by name in an Assessment of 1291 in connection with the medieval Church of Allhallows, which stood at its High Street corner until 1906. It shows how early the street had acquired its name from goldsmiths who resided there together. It is also interesting to note that it was, aptly, in Goldsmith Street (at Taylors' Hall) that the Exeter Company of Goldsmiths and Silversmiths had their first meeting on 1 August 1701. This was before they had obtained their own premises for meetings and assaying.

Allhallows Church

The city was empowered to remove Allhallows Church by the Exeter Corporation Act of 1900. The demolition of the church was referred to by a contemporary in 1906 as 'The latest sacrifice to the cry of 'street improvement.' We change little!

After the demolition of the church, Goldsmith Street, which had been extremely narrow, was widened to the width of what remains of it at its junction with High Street, between what were Horne's and Walton's premises. So the site of this tiny church (its nave was 23ft wide, and the width of its chancel, which formed the street corner, was only 11ft) is where the road and footpath are today.

Allhallows, which consisted of a chancel and a nave separated by a fourteenth-century arch, was offered for sale during the Commonwealth, and bought for £50 by a parishioner to rescue it from demolition. It was reopened in 1680 but by the early nineteenth century, again disused as a church, the building was described as 'dirty and in bad repair within'. Then in 1820 the City Chamber obtained an Act of Parliament for the removal of the church. However, it was once more saved from demolition, but two years later its sixteenth-century tower – which had been considerably reduced in height some 50 years earlier – was taken down. It had often been in need of repair and was a source of worry to the

Allhallows Church, at the corner of Goldsmith Street and High Street, was demolished in 1906.

church authorities. At the same time, a skylight in the roof of the nave was inserted, and after some restoration the church was reopened.

Some drawings of the last century show an interesting difference in this Goldsmith Street–High Street corner between its aspect when a seventeenth-century house built against the church was still there, until about 1880, and its appearance after that date when the old house was demolished and only the church formed the corner.

The very narrow gabled four-storey house, which had a late-eighteenth or early-nineteenth-century shop front, was said to have been built in 1618. The building, including this tiny shop (of a chemist) embraced the 'south' and 'east' walls of the chancel so that all that was visible of the church from High Street was one half of its chancel gable, with only the upper part of the 'east window' showing, the rest being concealed by the shop. Between the top of the house and the bay-window of the adjoining building, could also be seen part of the gable of the nave, and what remained of the tower.

This encroachment over the church may have, in some ways, been regrettable, but there is no doubt that the intricate and varied lines, the recesses and protrusions, formed by the mingling of these buildings, created an interesting and attractive visual effect. The seventeenth-century house had some historical interest too in that a Member of Parliament who was twice Lord Mayor of London had, as a youth, learnt his business as a druggist in its tiny shop (its width at no point exceeded 8ft!). He was Sir Matthew Wood.

The interior of Allhallows Church, Goldsmith Street.

After the house was demolished, the north-east side of Goldsmith Street (past the church) was set back. This, incidentally, freed the 'west end' of the church. The Victorian houses which faced the present square at the end of Waterbeer Street, and which have been demolished in the Marks & Spencer site development, were built at the time of this street widening in the 1880s.

There is a record in a contemporary guide to local traders, published in 1890, according to which the four-storey, gabled, bay-windowed house, which was No. 23/24, had been erected a few years earlier by a Mr J. Lock, a baker, pastrycook and confectioner, who also had a business in Sidwell Street. 'The lofty edifice is composed of red brick and dressed stone, and approaching it from Waterbeer Street presents a very fine view.' The shop front was surmounted by a wide arch, and the surrounding of the small, oval window above the entrance to the upper floors was decorated with scrolls, but these premises having been acquired by Walton in 1926, the shop window was eventually completely altered. About Mr Lock's shop the guidebook also states, '[it] is beautifully fitted with walnut and pitch pine and being surrounded by mirrors has a charming appearance. Coloured glass is also introduced into the windows and fanlights.' The floors above were 'designed for the accommodation of more than one family and shut

No. 22 Goldsmith Street (from the 1880s until 1974 the premises of Lear, Browne & Dunsford, the Woollen Merchants), one of the buildings whose façades were to be retained. They were swept away in the construction of the new Marks & Spencer premises.

off into two complete residential sets.'

All the other buildings on this side, except the market, also dated from after the widening of this part of Goldsmith Street. They all, no doubt, replaced houses which had been far more picturesque, but the Victorian buildings also had their charm, particularly No. 22 (the premises, until 1974, of Lear, Browne & Dunsford, the woollen merchants) sometimes known as Wool Hall, and No. 25, which had been the Phoenix Inn until it became an extension of Walton's in 1956.

The Wool Hall's façade was faced with heavily rusticated blocks of Beer stone and had round-headed window openings and doorways. At first-floor level, a row of balusters all along the width of the building, was divided into equal parts by six medallions. This arrangement of balusters, and blank panels above them, gave a pleasing impression of balconies and windows below the sloping slate roof. The woodwork of the interior, in the form of panelled doors, doorways, counters and shelves, was the best the Victorian age could produce.

What had been the Phoenix Inn, had a decorated gable surmounted by a finial, and a first-floor window within a large, ribbed arch, above which spandrels were adorned with figures. It was an unusual little building.

Robert Dymond, writing in 1884 in the *Exeter & Plymouth Daily Gazette*, mentions a mural tablet in Allhallows Church which recorded the death in 1817 of one Thomas Brown. He was apparently an eccentric character whose business premises were a warehouse on the upper floor of the High Street house next to the church and which was reached from the main street by a narrow way called Excise Passage. Brown, a native of Nottingham, was a hosier whose trade depended on private connections. 'There are some who can just remember him as an old bachelor

Top: *The original elevation of the Goldsmith Street entrance to the Higher Market, and* (above) *the altered façade now fronting the square which replaces Goldsmith Street.*

in a cocked hat, one of whose eccentricities consisted in offering to each customer a lemon cake just as other tradesmen of those days offered a dram.'

In the 1880s, James Crocker, an architect, and the author of *Sketches of Old Exeter*, was in charge of the restoration of the interior of Allhallows Church and of that of the exterior of its chancel. The church had been threatened with demolition again! But it was pulled down 20 years later when, according to contemporary opinion, it was 'in a very good state of

The ancient Goldsmith Street in 1979.

Goldsmith Street, 1979, the only building left standing.

High street frontages.

The Waltons premises, which extended over the years along High Street, Queen Street and Goldsmith Street. This old firm was closed in 1975 and the large area cleared and developed by Marks and Spencer.

Goldsmith Street (between Waterbeer Street and Paul Street) before its obliteration in the making of the Guildhall Centre.

Details of demolished Goldsmith Street buildings.

The houses facing the Guildhall Square, whose façades Marks & Spencer had expressed their willingness to preserve, were all demolished. (J.W.)

repair'. Its carved Tudor pulpit, mural tablets, and floor slabs were taken to St Pancras Church nearby, and the remains of people buried at Allhallows were transferred to the Higher Cemetery.

When the church was demolished in 1906, so that Goldsmith Street could be widened, the house in which Thomas Brown had had his warehouse became the corner house. Its Goldsmith Street frontage was in line with the fronts of the Wool Hall, Mr Lock's cake shop, and the Phoenix Inn, all built some 20 years earlier.

By 1906, the house in which Brown had carried on his trade was the warehouse of the Public Benefit Boot Company, and after 1911, it became that of Lennards, the boot manufacturers. The rebuilding of the premises probably dates from this period. By 1934 Walton's wool department occupied the corner (No. 26 Goldsmith Street). That firm, which had started business at 215–16 High Street early in this century, had extended over the years along Goldsmith Street, High Street, and Queen Street. Sadly, this local departmental store had to close in 1975. The site is being developed by Marks & Spencer.

The other side of Goldsmith Street, between High Street and Waterbeer Street, also witnessed the rise and fall of a local firm. Robert Howell, a draper, who already had his business at No. 206 High Street in 1853, was later joined by a partner, and the firm became Howell & Knapman. By 1878 they had extended their premises to include No. 207 High Street. Three years later, Edward Knapman was on his own and had acquired No. 1 Goldsmith Street. By 1928 the firm's premises extended into Goldsmith Street as far as Waterbeer Street, but 18 years later it closed down, and in 1949 Horne Bros moved in.

In 1881, in Goldsmith Street, there were two butchers, two engraver-printers, a basket maker, three refreshment houses, a builder, a locksmith, a newsagent, a baker, a dairy, a grocer, a poulterer, a jeweller, and three inns. The kind and number of trades had changed little towards the end of the century, but by 1906, at the time of the demolition of Allhallows Church, a point was made that fewer people lived in the area than had done previously, a number of them having moved to the suburbs. Then, when much of Paul Street was demolished in the 1920s, many of its inhabitants were rehoused further away from the centre.

These changes would account for the difference in the types of businesses in Goldsmith Street by 1939. There were at that time a draper, a departmental store, a hairdresser, bonded stores, leather merchants, woollen merchants, a refreshment house, an hotel, and two inns. By then, the oldest and most picturesque part of the street (which was opposite the market, between Waterbeer Street and Paul Street) stood almost empty, having lost its small trades. The Market Inn, No. 5, at the corner of Waterbeer Street, would still be there for another four years, and next to it, was Miss Gooden's refreshment house. While at the Paul Street end, Nos. 13 and 14 were respectively occupied by the Bull Hotel and J.H. Wills, a hairdresser. Between them, six lots of premises were unoccupied.

Then came the air raid of May 1942, and traders who had been bombed out of their shops in other parts of the city soon filled these places, and thus settled in Goldsmith Street, some for over 20 years as it turned out. By 1943, along this short stretch of an ancient street, there were four butchers consecutively (Stillmans, Boon, Havill and Eastmans) thus, by fate, recreating a pattern of the past when people of the same trade had gathered together in one street. The other food shops, past the butchers, had become occupied by the International Stores; Darch, the greengrocers; F. Cooper, the confectioner; Patch, another butcher; and the Holm Farm Dairy. Lyon, the jeweller; and Burgess, the ironmonger, also had premises then in this part of the street.

St Paul's Church

Past the market, and forming the corner of Goldsmith Street with Paul Street, stood until 1936 the Church of St Paul, which is said to have been dedicated, not to the Apostle, but to Paul, Bishop of Leon (an ancient region of Brittany), who died in 572. Little is known of the medieval church, for it had been completely rebuilt in the last quarter of the seventeenth century in the Renaissance style. The original outer walls were retained, but raised to a higher level, and new windows were inserted. The division between nave and aisles was removed and a new roof covered the whole width of the church. Inside, there was a screen, and an oak staircase gave access to a gallery at the west end, from which it was possible to see the original arches that carried the tower. The tower had acquired a window in the eighteenth century, which

St. Paul's Church (demolished 1936) stood in Paul Street at the corner of Goldsmith Street, seen here in its entirety. Typical of Old Exeter, this picturesque little street should have been preserved rather than demolished.

was probably put in when the gallery was added.

From the mid-1830s, when the market and Queen Street were being built, St Paul's Church had been hemmed in on its 'south' side by the market, and at its 'east end' by the market and other buildings. The church had a doorway into the tower from its 'west end' in Goldsmith Street, and its 'north' side fronted Paul Street. On this side were four high, round-headed windows, and exactly between them, a door gave access to the church.

Here several floor slabs recorded that members of the Gandy family had been buried in the church, including William Gandy, the gifted painter, who died on 14 July 1729 and who, it was believed, would have achieved lasting fame if he had been capable of more sustained work. Other members of the Gandy family were buried at Allhallows Church.

As we have seen in the chapter on Gandy Street, it owes its name to that family, who had, at some time, a house there, in the parish of St Paul. Before Queen Street was made, in the mid-1830s, the Paul Street end of Goldsmith Street was linked to Gandy Street by a narrow way, called Carey Lane until fairly late in the eighteenth century. What we call Upper Paul Street is what remains of it, and it gives some idea of the original lane.

When St Paul's Church was demolished, its memorials were transferred to St Martin's Church, and its screen to Honiton's own St Paul's Church. As for the remains of 306 people buried at the Exeter church, in accordance with a Home Office order, they had to be transferred to a new burial place at night and under secrecy. And so, in the early hours of 25 April 1936, not even the Police were aware of the movements of a gruesome convoy of lorries, containing black boxes bearing only white identification numbers, whose destination was a mass grave at the Higher Cemetery. The whole operation took place by the light of hurricane lamps. Later in the day, a service was held at the grave by the Rector of St Paul's. A plan had been made to record the exact position in the church where the individual remains were found.

Some 30 years earlier, when other features in the city had already vanished, and the quaint little Allhallows Church was pulled down, a local architect wrote to the *Church Times*, 'Formerly an exceedingly picturesque city, Exeter is now but a sha dow of what it formerly was.'

Sources
Beatrix Cresswell (1908), *Exeter Churches*
Alexander Jenkins (1806), *History of the City of Exeter*
H. Tapley-Soper, *Parishes of Allhallows and St Paul* (For the Devon and Cornwall Record Society, 1928)
Articles in *Exeter & Plymouth Daily Gazette* (Robert Dymond, November 1883 to July 1884)
Letter in *Western Morning News*, 18 January 1932
Nineteenth-century drawings, before and after 1880, of Allhallows, photographs of Allhallows (1906); of St Paul's (1926)
James Crocker, *Sketches of Old Exeter*
Where to Buy (a local trades guide, published 1890)
City Directories from 1853

The Paul Street multi-storey car park and the Cathedral!

Multi-storey car parks, illustrating the insensitive reconstruction of Paul Street and Bartholomew Street.

Paul Steet multi-storey car park (part of the Guildhall Centre) as seen from the Rougemont Hotel.

The Paul Street ramp to the Guildhall Centre car park obscures the sight of fine buildings in Queen Street and beyond.

The north side of Waterbeer Street showing the 1887 Police Station, demolished in the early 1960s.

The same side of the street in 1979.

✦ CHAPTER 25 ✦

The Guildhall Centre and St Pancras Church

That Exeter was going to have a delightful new city centre, was the conviction derived from an illustrated report submitted in December 1969 to Exeter City Council by the Consultants Hugh Wilson and Lewis Wolmersley.

For instance, according to the recommendations and illustrations in this report, when coming out of the High Street arcade into the Guildhall precinct, we were to be in full view of the whole south side of St Pancras Church. Also, Waterbeer Street was to have a generously sized space provided with trees, an attractive paving, and an interesting variety of new buildings whose roof lines and slightly different heights would create a pleasing geometry. The most important consideration here was to have reserved a place of honour for the small thirteenth-century church of St Pancras. The intention was that it would be surrounded by adequate space, no other building being very near it. In short, the new Guildhall Centre was going to be a marvellous example of how to make the new fit the old, and to distribute the space between them to the greatest advantage of both.

But in the early 1970s, the city council negotiated with a development company and two years later this company was granted full planning consent for the scheme which was completed in November 1976. It is a perfect example of the manner in which good projects can be abandoned in favour of inferior ones.

True, the Guildhall Centre has enclosures, arcades and little odd corners that are pleasing enough to walk through because they give a feeling of intimacy and security: nothing is out of scale and no vehicle can run us over. The actual shopping there is convenient too, and the sheltered areas are appreciated when it rains.

But visually, the scheme is a failure because what had originally been intended to remain just space has been filled; because the design of all the new buildings in this centre is uniform and very poor; and because a fine nineteenth-century building, meant to be an important feature in the complex, has lost much of its elevation in the considerable raising of the ground in front of it, and thus acquired a squat appearance.

Roof-top view from Richmond Road, overlooking the centre of the City, c.1960.

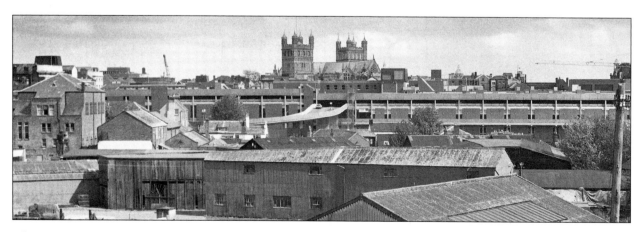

The extensive structure which forms the Paul Street side of the Guildhall Centre.

Early-seventeenth-century chimney-piece preserved in a jeweller's shop, part of the Guildhall Precinct.

Above: *This building, once the premises of E.I. Munk, the Ironmonger, formed part of a well-restored group in Waterbeer Street.*

Right: *The interior of Munk's shop, Waterbeer Street.*

Restored buildings of Waterbeer Street, 1979.

St Pancras Church before restoration.

The interior of St Pancras Church showing the Jacobean pulpit once in the Church of Allhallows, Goldsmith Street.

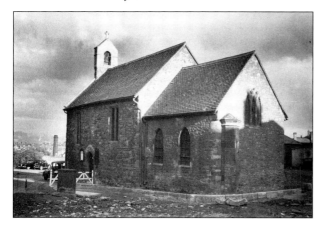

The thirteenth-century church of St Pancras stood in the ancient lane of St Pancras (obliterated in the construction of the Guildhall Centre)

The generous space in Waterbeer Street, within which trees could have grown, has, in the developers' scheme, shrunk to a narrow way by the addition of buildings. They create a massive screen which prevents the church from being seen until one is very close to it.

The Consultants had also intended the delightful little church of St Pancras itself to be surrounded by decent space, but the developers' dreary buildings now squat in jarring proximity to it.

As we have seen in previous chapters, the façade of the old market in the precinct lost its fine proportion and much of its elegance when the ground was raised in front of it, and it became tastelessly attached to uncomely new buildings on either side. The Consultants had also suggested good quality materials, including brick, for the paving of the precinct. Artificial stone of nondescript colour, which breaks easily, has been used instead.

The new buildings entirely lack variety and suitability for the site. They are monotonously of identical height; they have unbroken, horizontal roof lines and flat façades without recesses or protrusions; and the materials used are dully smooth red brick, dirty-white concrete and dark-grey pseudo-slate. The

latter, covering the top of buildings, makes them look as if they were wearing monstrous helmets. Nearly all the windows are of the sash variety and oblong.

These new structures stand there in dull contrast to the buildings which have been retained on one side of Waterbeer Street and whose gables of various shapes and sizes, hand-made bricks, coarse red sandstone and stuccoed walls, all form a pleasing mixture of line, colour and texture. Until recently, the buildings of Goldsmith Street were another interesting side of this Waterbeer Street square, but they have now all been demolished.

Once, Waterbeer Street was a complete street from North Street to Goldsmith Street, which as we have seen in another chapter, was also a complete street. St Pancras Church was in Pancras Lane, which joined Waterbeer Street to Paul Street.

In December 1934, members of Exeter City Council were rather worried, being faced with the possibility of the council acquiring St Pancras Church. The problem had arisen because the local authority wanted then, 45 years ago, to rebuild the area behind the Guildhall, and consequently a Corporation Bill was before Parliament in which the city was given the power to acquire St Pancras. Although the council did not want the church, the fear of being hampered in its project had been the reason for seeking that power.

Eventually, the problem was solved when the city and ecclesiastical authorities agreed that the former would make no claim on the church, if the latter did not interfere 'with the laying out of the new streets in the area... provided that suitable access was given to the church.'

However, although the demolition of some property took place round the church (which had to be stayed while work was in progress) the new layout and reconstruction had to wait some 40 years.

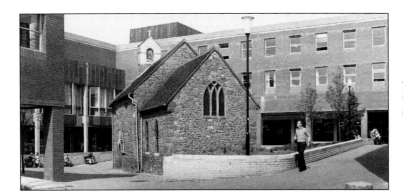

Insensitive planning resulted in the erection of new buildings much too close to the church.

It is not clear to which of two saints of the same name St Pancras Church was dedicated. Pancras of Rome is said to have been a Phrygian orphan brought by his uncle to Rome where both were converted to Christianity, and Pancras died as a martyr at the age of 14, in the early-fourth century. Relics of this Pancras were sent by the Pope to the King of Northumbria in the seventh century. Six ancient churches in England were dedicated to St Pancras of Rome, including one in London from which the cemetery and the railway station took their name. Pancras of Taormina is reputed to have been sent to Sicily as a missionary by St Peter in the first century. There, he was stoned to death. Ten English churches were dedicated to him and it is thought that this may have been due to the close contact in the twelfth century between Norman England and Sicily, which by 1091 had been conquered by the Normans.

The earliest mention of the Exeter church of St Pancras is in a surviving document of 1191, but although some nineteenth-century work on the church revealed an early doorway in the south wall of the chancel (Saxon or Norman) the church as we see it today is in the Early English style of the thirteenth century. It consists of a chancel and a nave, and the whole building is only 46ft by 16ft.

It is an attractive little building in shape, proportion, colour and texture. It was built of the purple, volcanic stone from Northernhay, and the surrounds and mullions of the windows are also made of volcanic stone, but there are other local stones in the building, of various sizes and shapes, which give its walls an attractive texture and colour: white-veined volcanic Pocombe stone, coarse Heavitree sandstone, and a smooth type of red sandstone.

The tracery of the East window and the lancet windows in the chancel are all typical of the thirteenth century. In the small turret at the west end of the church is a bell said to have been made in Exeter by Robert Newton in the mid-fifteenth century. Its Latin inscription, loosely translated into English, is, 'I may be small but I am well heard over a wide area.'

To enter the church now gives a shock. The kind of ground surface or floor covering which joins a wall is extremely important to the appearance of this wall. For instance, good tiles or flagstones laid up to the walls of a house improve its appearance; tarmac

would ruin it. Many such 'points of Junction' are catastrophic.

What shocks as one enters St Pancras Church today is the sight of a floor covering more suited to a supermarket or a cafe than to the interior of a medieval building. Vinyl floors were never meant to join thirteenth-century stone walls. This, with the dazzlingly white partition at the west end of the nave, and waiting-room chairs around the walls, distract uncomfortably from such unobtrusive features as medieval stoup, piscina, doorway and stairs (once to the rood loft), and look remarkably gaudy beside the patina of the Norman font and Jacobean pulpit. The latter came to St Pancras in 1906 when Allhallows, Goldsmith Street, was demolished.

The interior of St Pancras Church was described early in the nineteenth century as 'dark and gloomy', and another comment was, 'As no use is now made of this church, excepting as a cemetery for a few families, it is consequently very much neglected, and may soon be desecrated.' But the church was restored in the 1830s, and again some 50 years later.

In spite of its failure architecturally, its wrong distribution of space and buildings, and the reckless demolition which it has involved, and which, in Goldsmith Street, continues (March 1979), we can be thankful that we have this Guildhall Centre, not the one that the Council's Planning Department had envisaged in 1961 and which would have caused the demolition, within the area surrounded by Paul Street, North Street, High Street and Queen Street, of every single building except the Guildhall, the Turk's Head and St.' Pancras Church!

Sources
David Hugh Farmer (1978), *The Oxford Dictionary of Saints*
Alexander Jenkins (1806), *History of the City of Exeter*
Beatrix Cresswell (1908), *Exeter Churches*
Re Council project for area at the back of the Guildhall (*Western Morning News*, December 19, 1934)
H. Tapley-Soper (1933), *The Parish of St. Pancras*, for the Devon & Cornwall Record Society
Report on Redevelopment of Guildhall Area (Hugh Wilson & Lewis Womersley, Chartered Architects & Town Planners, December, 1969)

✦ CHAPTER 26 ✦

The Two Sides of Catherine Street

(St Catherine's Almshouses, The Annuellars' College, St Stephen's Church

In spite of bomb damage in the last war, the pleasingly narrow Catherine Street, with its medieval ruins, St Stephen's Church, and an attractive little square between them, retains some charm and is enjoyable to walk through.

A wall had been erected around the cathedral after the murder in 1285 of a member of its Chapter, and St Catherine's Gate was one of the seven gates in this wall, giving access to the precinct. A ring in the wall opposite the nearby ruins still shows where the gate stood.

At right-angles with Catherine Street, in line with St Stephen's Bow and the side of the ruined chapel, used to be an ancient lane known as Egypt (later, Chapel Lane) which led to the city wall. In 1297, Edward I had ordered the cathedral clergy to allow the use of the lane, and free access to the city wall, to those citizens responsible for its maintenance. Part of this lane was still in existence before the bombing of 1942. Its site is now (1979) a private car park.

The ruins in Catherine Street are confusing – and the plaque there does not help – because they appear to be of the same original foundation. It is a pity that in the laying out of this area in 1959, part of the wall between the two lots of ruins, which was a remaining part of the thirteenth-century cathedral boundary wall, was demolished, but we must be thankful that what was left of these historical buildings after the air raids of 1942 was kept, and that a pleasant little garden was made around them.

The western part of these ruins is what remains of the Annuellars' College, founded in the fourteenth century just within the cathedral precinct; the adjoining ruins on the eastern side, are the remains of St Catherine's Almshouses, founded in the fifteenth century on the other side of the cathedral boundary wall. What is left of the College is mostly part of the kitchen. As in all kitchens of fairly large establishments, there would have been a boiling hearth and a roasting hearth, these two fireplaces can still be seen, each with its bread oven. One of the walls of the kitchen is mostly made up of the type of volcanic stone found in the buildings of Exeter until the end of the fourteenth century.

The College occupied a fairly extensive site. It is said that there was an entrance in the Close, opposite the north door of the cathedral, as well as in Catherine Street. In 1915, a large workshop on an adjoining site, west of the ruins, was thought to have been the Annuellars' hall. Three arched doorways at the end of the hall might well have led, respectively, to a pantry, a buttery, and to the kitchen, the usual arrangement for medieval domestic quarters. Unfortunately, the wall, with its three telling doorways, was demolished in 1959 when the ruins were tidied up and the garden was made. There has been since 1966 a low building on the site.

The name 'Annuellars' derives from the fact that

Old Catherine Street, c.1890.

Catherine Street 1979.

The north side of Catherine Street, late-nine-teenth-century, where Colson's premises were later erected.

Nineteenth-century demolition on the south side of Catherine Street, next to St Martin's Church.

the members of the College, who were attached to the cathedral, celebrated masses annually, on the anniversary of the death of people who had left money for that purpose. Part of the buildings of the Annuellars' College had been adapted for use as the Country House Inn. It was destroyed in the air attack of May 1942.

St Catherine's Almshouses were built in 1457 on a waste piece of land, after a petition – still in existence – for a licence to found them, had been addressed to Henry VI by Canon John Stevens. The almshouses, consisting of 13 rooms and a chapel, were for the benefit of 13 poor men. Most of what remains was the chapel, and until the last war it had a wagon roof.

In the seventeenth century the chapel was no longer used as such, and the upper and ground floors were divided into cottages for poor people. By the early-nineteenth century, it was used as a carpenter's workshop, but in 1897 the buildings were taken over by the Church Army and used as a hostel for men until they became ruins in the last war's bombing.

The chapel is built of local (Heavitree) red sandstone, so widely used in Exeter from the fifteenth century to the nineteenth. The four walls, window openings and doorway, are all that is left of the chapel; the wall with window openings in it along Catherine Street, and the wall which forms a right-angle with it, were part of the poor men's houses.

On the eastern side of St Stephen's Church, once stood the New Inn, whose attractive front, casement windows, and ornamented cornice are shown in an engraving of St Stephen's Bow by W.H. Sweet. The inn had been erected in the fifteenth century on land belonging to the Dean and Chapter of Exeter Cathedral, and had acquired, by the seventeenth

century, its famous Apollo Room, whose beautiful plaster ceiling could still be seen after the First World War on what, by then, were the premises of the drapers Green & Son.

Before the last war, a covered passageway along the south side of St Stephen's Church led to an entrance into Bobby's shop (which in those days adjoined Colson's); it was destroyed in the air raid of May 1942 and the church also suffered.

An incendiary bomb set fire to the interior of the tower, which caused its three bells to fall to the ground – the pieces were later melted to make one new bell – and the famous 'Bow' was also damaged. This is the part which forms an archway leading from Catherine Street to High Street; from the interior of the church, this was reached by a dignified flight of steps at the east end and which originally contained a chapel dedicated to St John the Evangelist. In recent years, alterations, some for the convenience of the lay functions of the church, have resulted in partitions being erected to form a vestry at the west end; a kitchen on the north side; and the separation from the main body of the church of the Bow, which is now reached by narrow, enclosed steps leading to a locked door. The church has consequently lost some of the character it had retained until 1942.

St Stephen's Church is mentioned in the Domesday Book, and in 1222, when parish boundaries were defined and the number of parish churches in Exeter fixed at 19, St Stephen's became one of them. It has had since a very eventful life.

In 1658, the year of Cromwell's death, the church was sold for £250 to one Toby Allen who used its crypt as a stable. The tower was partly pulled down, and the church so badly treated that it had to be

An ancient lane called 'Egypt' (later Chapel Lane) beside St Catherine's Almshouses.

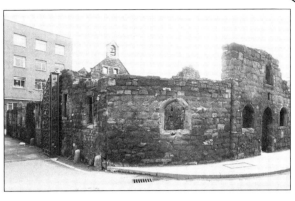

The site in the early 1980s.

St Catherine's Almshouses after the air raid of 1942. The building was used at the time by the Church Army.

The ruins of St Catherine's Almshouses and the Annuellars' College.

St. Stephens bow and (right) the New Inn, c.1900.

St. Stephen's church, High Street.

The Apollo Room and its plaster ceiling were a seven-teenth-century addition at 'The New Inn'. The ceiling could still be seen in the 1920s on the premises of Green & Son (drapers), later acquired by Bobby's.

Green & Son (drapers) Nos. 25–26 High Street.

Post-war rebuilding of Colson's (later Dingles).

rebuilt when it was recovered by the parish at the Restoration of the monarchy. A certain George Potter, 'Merchant and Alderman', who died in 1662, has a monument in St Stephen's which records that he was a 'great benefactor to the rebuilding of the church.' But while repairs were carried out, the building was totally destroyed by fire. The oldest parts of the present church, as seen from the outside, date from its complete rebuilding in 1664.

Although their war-damaged tracery has been renewed, part of the stone work of the windows dates from that period. Bricks with facing of crushed (Heavitree) red sandstone were used in repair work to the walls.

To the south of the Bow outside, traces in the church wall show where the east window used to be. Below, a filled-in round-headed doorway is thought to have been once an entrance to the crypt. The tower and turret had to be rebuilt after the war, and the concrete repair to the battlements on the north side of the church is very obvious.

In 1826 the city chamber had served a notice on St Stephen's wardens that the tower must be removed or repaired. It was repaired. But the church was mortgaged for £100, and the whole of its interior was completely rebuilt. It was then that the medieval crypt under it was rediscovered. Contemporary descriptions of its two columns indicate that the crypt dated from not later than the twelfth century. The crypt was eventually closed again, and even the stone which showed where it was found in 1826, has now been concealed.

The present interior of the church, apart from alterations made after the last war, is that of the early-nineteenth century. The clustered shafts of the columns, with their circular, moulded capitals, recall the thirteenth-century Gothic. They support Tudor-style arches and form two aisles. Until the last war, two now filled-in arches behind the altar had below

them, respectively, the flight of steps leading up to the altar in St Stephen's Bow, and a picture of the Woman of Samaria. A dado in the wall of the south and north aisles show where the box pews were, and there was also a gallery in the church between 1772 and 1895.

Other events connected with this church were its near-destruction in 1894 (it was saved because repair was found to be cheaper than demolition and reconstruction), and offers made by business firms in 1930 and since the last war, to buy it in order to pull it down and build their own premises on the site!

Sources

E. Lega Weekes, *Studies in the Topography of the Cathedral Close*
J. Davidson, MSS on Exeter churches
Beatrix Cresswell, *Exeter Churches*
R.K. Sledge, *St Stephen's Church*
Newspaper reports relating to war damage in Exeter.

CHAPTER 27

The Destroyed Centre of Exeter
– High Street –

That pre-war stretch of High Street which stood between the present premises of Boots and St Stephen's Church, and which was badly damaged in the air raid of May 1942, and later, with its road pattern, undiscernedly destroyed, had been a part of the city full of interest and variety.

Its width was that of what remains of this pre-war street between St Stephen's Church and the junction South Street–North Street, and its buildings, which differed in height enough to create variety, but not so much as to be incongruous, were also varied in shape, several being gabled, others having parapets above their cornices. Some of these buildings had sash windows; a few had casement and bay windows. The eye could rove and find on both sides of the street a pleasing mixture of lines and angles created by a diversity of roofs and façades.

The High Street postwar dual carriageway was made considerably wider than the original road (although since it has been, in recent years, closed to all traffic except buses, it has now been shrunk to a narrow channel). The pavement on the north side is inordinately wide, and we can see how much further back the present buildings are than the pre-war ones were, if we consider the angle formed by Curry's and the side of what was Lyons' premises until fairly recently.

The junction of Bedford Street with High Street is also wider than it was, the buildings forming the two new corners having been erected further apart than the pre-war ones were.

It is interesting to remember some of the buildings and businesses which were in that part of High Street before it was so badly maimed, and then irrevocably destroyed.

Next to the Cooperative Society premises (which were spared by the bombing, escaped reconstruction, and date from the 1930s) was the very exclusive dress shop of Joan Cresswell. It must be said though that it was more highly rated for the quality of its customers and clothes than for the chic of its styles. Between Joan Cresswell's shop and the National Provincial Bank was the entrance to the Arcade.

This linked High Street to Southernhay, and was approximately on the site of the short pedestrian way which starts opposite Boots at East Gate House, and runs past the Gas Board showrooms. It had been built in 1882 and was a typical Victorian arcade, with a glass roof, and full of fascinating shops such as, Towill, 'goldsmiths, silversmiths and watchmakers'; Melhuish, 'art furnishers'; E. Stacey, 'antiques'; Chandler, 'photographers'; Culme Weave, 'knitwear specialist'; W. Rayner, 'fancy draper and furrier'; Barns and Van Houten, 'milliners'; R.H. Cummings,

A unique photographic record! Exeter Cathedral lit by incendiary bombs during the Blitz, 1942.

High Street as seen from The London Inn Square, c.1930), with the General Post Office (left) next to the National Provincial Bank.

The statue of Henry VII had stood over the East Gate until its demolition in 1784.

The entrance to the High Street Arcade, built in 1882.

The interior of the High Street Arcade.

Pre-war High Street. Boots's premises are now partly on the site of Mark Rowe seen here on the right.

Pre-war High Street. The Commercial Union premises are now on the site of St Lawrence's Church (right).

Lloyds Bank, High Street, is now on the site of the Commercial Union Assurance Co. (left).

'umbrella manufacturers', etc. Within the Arcade too, was the entrance to the Underground Passages.

On the same side of High Street, past the Arcade and the bank, stood the General Post Office, which had moved from its Queen Street premises to its new site in 1885. Among other firms, between the bank and Bampfylde Street, were Payn (where one could buy the best coffee in Exeter); A Lewis, the tobacconists; E. Sebley, 'hosier, hatter, and glover'; Troulans, the opticians; Wynne Tighe & Son, the chemists; Mrs Marsden's 'ladies' and servants' registry'; Mac Fisheries; and Havill & Son, the butchers.

Bampfylde Street joined High Street practically where the present Arcade does, so that narrow, picturesque, little street was in a straight line with Castle Street. Between the junctions of High Street with, respectively, Bampfylde Street and Bedford Street, were some 15 different kinds of businesses. Among them, two cafes, a tailor, a silk and wool hosiery and underwear specialist, two insurance companies, an umbrella shop, and a bank. At Berni's Continental Café, one could savour delicious mixed grills and drink the only good coffee supplied by a restaurant or café in Exeter before the war.

Barclays Bank occupied a similar position to that which it does today, bearing in mind that the pre-war

High Street, c.1930, with St Stephen's church on the right.

corners Higher Street–Bedford Street were not exactly on the same sites as the present ones. Buildings occupied a larger site in High Street between Bedford Street and St Stephen's Church than they do today. Those people who rebuilt Exeter seem

St Lawrence's Church after the air raid of 1942. The site was occupied by the Commercial Union.

High Street after the air raid of 1942. Taken from the top of the General Post Office.

The junction of High Street with Bedford Street after the air raid of 1942, but before the demolition of these buildings was completed.

High Street and its junction with Bedford Street as demolition squads complete the destruction of the buildings.

Castle Street in the early 1950s. The site is being cleared for the erection of Marks & Spencer's premises.

Left: *High Street buildings next to St Stephen's Church survived the war and were replaced by the Dingle premises (once Colsons).*

An aerial view of Exeter during its reconstruction, c.1955.

to have preferred motor vehicles and roads to buildings, and so Bedford Street, as well as High Street, was considerably widened. It is ironical that these are now pedestrian areas!

The present corner formed by Manfield, the shoe shop, is somewhat to the west of the pre-war corner which was formed by Lloyds Bank on the ground floor and the fabulous café–restaurant, Dellers, up above, these premises extending considerably along both Bedford Street and High Street.

People coming to Exeter some time after its air raid of May 1942, thought that the razing to the ground of a vast area of the city was entirely due to 'enemy action'. They were mistaken. Some of our photographs show, typically, what happened to several buildings which could have been saved. One photograph shows the corners Bedford Street–High Street with Barclays Bank, Lloyds Bank, and Dellers, with part of their structure still sound. The round-headed window openings of Lloyds Bank and its entrance; the gables, most of the transomes and mullions of Dellers, and its two large Ionic columns supporting a vast entablature, were all still sound enough after the bombing to warrant repair to these buildings. The other photograph shows the same

part of High Street with these buildings in the process of being unnecessarily but officially and completely destroyed.

The store, Bobby – now absorbed by Debenham's – had until 1942 premises on both sides of St Stephen's Church. Its premises of Nos 25–26 High Street, which stood on the east side of the church, between it and Lloyds Bank, were completely destroyed during the air raid of 1942. Something new would have had to be built there, in keeping with what should have been preserved and repaired next door to it.

The other side of High Street (north), between Gandy Street and the present Boots's premises, also suffered much during the air raid of May 1942. We can trace, approximately, the sites of some of the pre-war buildings, but it has to be borne in mind that they were not set back as the new ones are, but were in line with those High Street buildings which are still between Queen Street and Gandy Street.

Among others here, past Lyons and A. Lewis, the tobacconist, was James Commin 'new and second-hand bookseller'. After the blitz, the firm moved to premises in the Cathedral Yard, in whose basement it was always sheer joy to discover on one of the

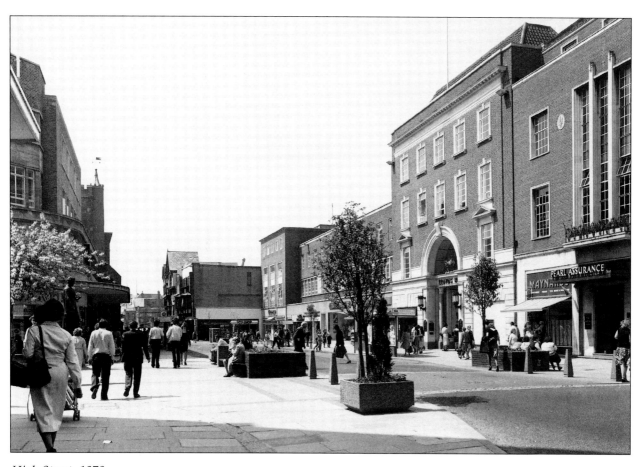

High Street, 1979.

High Street, 1979.

Princesshay, part of the rebuilt City Centre, 1979.

shelves surrounding the ancient well, perhaps a beautifully printed and illustrated book, lovingly written by some scholarly clergyman who had had much time on his hands in the last century.

Next to Commin,s in High Street, was A. Wheaton, 'stationers, booksellers and account book makers'. The firm still exists elsewhere in Exeter, but is no longer locally owned. Another well-known firm in those days, only four numbers further up the street, was Eland Bros, also booksellers and

stationers. Somewhere between these two booksellers was a narrow passageway called King's Alley in which were the Corporation of Exeter's 'tepid swimming baths'.

The Commercial Union Assurance was approximately on the site of the present Lloyds Bank building. That insurance company's High Street premises had been rebuilt in 1833 by the Devon architect Andrew Patey. This edifice had a splendid façade with Corinthian columns and an impressive

131

porch and entablature. Dominating it all was a statue of King Alfred on a plinth. (He had been the emblem of the West of England Fire and Life Insurance Co. which merged with the Commercial Union in 1894.) This fine façade and its royal adornment were not destroyed in the blitz. But only the head of King Alfred was preserved. It was later remounted and is displayed in the entrance of the Commercial Union's present premises. Since photographs taken after the bombing of May 1942 show the whole statue in its original position, at the top of the building, what is likely to have happened is that all of it except the head was carelessly broken in the course of the demolition of the façade, when all bombed buildings were being indiscriminately razed to the ground as the result of an official decision.

Next to the Commercial Union was an interesting group of bay-windowed, gabled houses, the premises of Brufords, the jewellers, Fred Ford, 'sign makers, fancy costumiers and hirers', and Wippel Bros & Row, 'manufacturing ironmongers'. The entrance to Musgrave's Alley between the latter and the former could easily be missed. The Devon and Somerset Store had an unusual Victorian façade with finials surmounting its roof parapet. Then, past a small building with a pyramidal slate roof, was the Church of St Lawrence.

Its site is now occupied by the Commercial Union's present premises. In a corner of the entrance, opposite King Alfred's bust, is a statue of Queen Elizabeth I. It was once on a conduit which bore the date 1590 and which had stood at the top of High Street. In 1694 the conduit was removed from the street and its materials were used to build a south porch to the church, against its tower. The statue of Queen Elizabeth was placed in a niche within the gable of the porch. It survived wartime enemy action in 1942, as did the church tower, the porch and some of the walls. Only the statue escaped the later, official destruction.

The tower of the church, whose string-course below its crenellation had interesting carvings including four angels at the corners, was thought by generations to be clumsy, ill-proportioned and too large for the church.

The earliest account of St Lawrence's dates from 1222, but the building which was destroyed 720 years later was Perpendicular Gothic in style, with typical fifteenth-century tracery to its windows. The little church had a barrel roof with coloured and gilded bosses carved with faces and foliage, and the wall plates were adorned with angels carrying shields. The east end of the church was described 70 years ago as having its nave and sanctuary divided by a fifteenth-century carved work with stalls. The carving was said to consist of clusters of small heads grouped round each pinnacle. There had been three bells in the tower but in 1780 two of them had to be sold to pay for repair work, so the church was left with one medieval bell.

Between St Lawrence's Church and Castle Street were the Empire cinema, a tobacconist, a hatter, the Electricity Co. and the Westminster Bank (on the present site of the National Westminster Bank); and between Castle Street and the site of the present Boots premises, were several shoe shops, hatters, dress shops, one leather shop, tailors, one umbrella shop, a chocolate shop, a tea merchant, a chemist, a furniture shop, jewellers and stationers.

One of these buildings, gabled, and low compared to the others, boasted the date 1297 on its façade. However, it looked a typical sixteenth- or early-seventeenth century house. But the most notable were Nos 266–67, the premises of Mark Rowe & Sons, a furniture shop. By the shop window was the elaborate plaque (now on the opposite side of High Street) which informed that the site had been that of the East Gate of the city.

Mark Rowe's building was remarkable because although Georgian in style (above the shop window) it had been built with the volcanic Northernhay stone of the medieval gate, after the latter was demolished in 1784, and because in a niche, specially made between the first-floor sash windows, was the statue of Henry VII which had stood over the gate until its demolition.

In the pre-war High Street, one could experience a certain well-being within its human scale, and looking at its small shops (nearly all the businesses of local people), a well-being of which we are now deprived as we walk along a very wide (often windy) street lined with almost identical buildings where very similar goods are sold by multiple shops.

Sources

Isca Collection of photographs (High Street section)
Besley's pre-war Directories of Exeter
Minutes of Exeter City Council (1942)
A. Jenkins (1806), *History and Description of the City of Exeter*
Beatrix Cresswell (1908), *Exeter Churches*
A.M. Shorto (1911), *The Story of Exeter*

CHAPTER 28

Bampfylde House

Before the obliteration of much of the original street pattern in the post-war reconstruction of Exeter, Catherine Street did not end at its junction with Bedford Street, but continued in a straight line on the other side of it, until it met Bampfylde Street at right-angles.

Bampfylde Street was a narrow, picturesque lane which joined Catherine Street to High Street, and started from this main street exactly opposite Castle Street. At the corner of Catherine Street and Bampfylde Street stood the lovely late-sixteenth-century Bampfylde House, one of the gems of the city, which was destroyed by fire in the air raid of May 1942. Its site is somewhere within the present High Street Arcade.

Bampfylde House, from the early-nineteenth century, had been used by various tenants, such as the 'Devon County Club for the Propagation of the Principles of the British Constitution and the Maintenance of Civil and Religious Liberty', and as offices. In 1913, the Russian Vice-Consulate was there, as well as the French Consular Agency. It was also the premises of Varwell, Guest & Co. Ltd, the coal and coke factors and colliery agents, who

purchased the house soon after the First World War from Lord Poltimore, to whose family it had belonged since the sixteenth century.

In 1929, Bampfylde House, which had been bought the previous year from his firm, by Arthur Guest, was let to an antique dealer, R.M.K. Buchanan, who arranged his finest collection of antiques in the beautifully panelled and ceilinged Jacobean solar. It is significant of the taste of Exonians at the time that the city counted some 40 antique shops!

Arthur Guest was both a man of taste and a city councillor. It was thanks to his interest in the house that coats of lateVictorian paint were removed from some of the walls, and that the fine oak panels and fireplace of the solar reappeared in all their splendour. He was later offered (but he refused) £6,500 for those panels alone, and he declined a generous offer for the whole house, so that the city could acquire it for £5,000, the price he had paid his firm for it five years earlier.

On 7 November 1934, Bampfylde House was opened to the public by the Mayor of Exeter. The house was suitably furnished by the city, partly with what could be found at the museum (a table came

Bampfylde House.

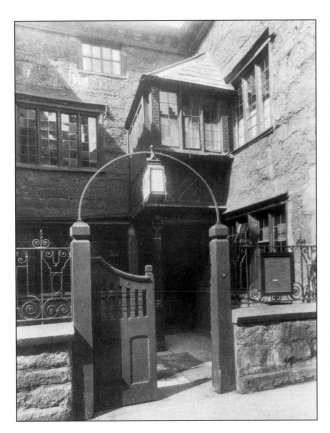

Entrance and porch to Bampfylde House.

Bampfylde House (late-sixteenth century), with (on the left) Old Catherine Street.

from an attic in the Guildhall), and partly with gifts sent by keen and generous people. An old iron-bound oak coffer, which had belonged to the wharfinger's office, was found in a store on the Quay. It had three compartments with corresponding locks and slots for the insertion of coins. While being cleaned and repaired, before being sent to Bampfylde House, it yielded a silver penny dating from 1547.

The Manor of Poltimore had been held by the Poltimore family for several generations when Sir Richard Poltimore, having no issue, granted it to Simon Lord Montacute. It changed hands again, and was acquired in 1298 by John Baunfeld or Bampfylde, whose family was already well established in the county. But it was not until over 500 years later that a Bampfylde became Lord Poltimore. This was when in 1831 Sir George Warwick Bampfylde was raised to the peerage and his manor gave its name to the new barony. One of his ancestors, Richard Bampfylde, had begun to build Bampfylde House as a town house in 1590, and although he died four years later, the work was completed by his son Amias.

Originally, the front of the house had been enclosed by 14ft-high walls forming a court, and there were no windows at ground-floor level on the other sides. The entrance was from Bampfylde Street – known until the mid-eighteenth century as Raden Lane – and in a corner of the quadrangle, formed by the two wings of the house, was a porch supported by moulded Jacobean oak posts, and surmounted, above a carved frieze, by a small room whose

window rested on carved brackets.

The porch opened into a large hall whose six-light mullioned window, in the centre of the house, bore fifteenth-century stained-glass armorials which referred to ancestors of the Bampfyldes and their wives. Facing this window, and reaching the ceiling, was once a magnificent chimney-piece. But it had been moved to Poltimore House after the death in 1814 of Georgina Sophia Bampfylde, the last member of the family to occupy Bampfylde House. The chimney-piece was moved again later to another Bampfylde property in North Molton. Below the hall, a large, original cellar could be reached from the paved court by a flight of stone steps.

In 1724, Sir Coplestone Warwick Bampfylde had removed the screens in the hall, as well as the Elizabethan staircase, replacing it with one of painted pine, but he left the sixteenth-century newel post which reached the top of the house. Over a door of the first-floor landing was a shield showing the impaled arms of the Bampfyldes and Cliftons: Elizabeth Clifton was the wife of Amias Bampfylde.

This door gave access to a large room, once the solar, but known later, when the house was open to the public, as the Oak Room. It was Amias who, after being knighted by James I in 1603, much enriched the house that his father had built. The walls of the solar were covered with carved oak panels; and above a wooden cornice, was an ornate plaster frieze. Over the richly decorated chimney-piece, Amias Bampfylde set up elaborate plaster work showing his family coat of arms quartered with that of his wife. It has been said that the magnificent ceiling in this room was part of the eighteenth-century alterations; this is most unlikely. The more simple, plaster ceilings in other rooms of this house were consistent with the late-sixteenth century; the sumptuous plaster work of the Oak Room ceiling was in keeping with the other ornate features in this room, and typical of the seventeenth century. The beautiful Oak Room had two three-light windows, one on either side of the chimney-piece, and a five-light oriel-

The Oak Room, Bampfylde House.

The Oak Room fireplace.

Detail of chimney piece in the Oak Room.

The Hall.

An Elizabethan bedroom.

Bampfylde House dining-room.

Bampfylde House kitchen.

Bampfylde House at the junction of Bampfylde Street with Old Catherine Street before and after the air raid of 1942.

window on the Bampfylde Street side of the house.

Five members of the Bampfylde family were several times Members of Parliament, and from 1654, Thomas Bampfylde, the youngest brother of Amias, was Recorder of the city for six years.

In 1730, when Bampfylde House was used for a time as a boarding-school, an announcement stated that the house had a good garden, clear air, and a prospect from the town walls. Gardens belonging to the house then extended eastward as far as the city wall. Later, this site was filled with stables, and later still, with the Bedford Garage. The site of these gardens is now part of Princesshay and of some of the shops on the east side of it.

Bampfylde House, until the dreadful night of its destruction, nearly 40 years ago, seems to have had an uneventful life, although it was involved in at least one exciting event, which was recorded.

In July 1769, the Duke of Bedford, being in Exeter to receive the freedom of the city, was, on leaving the Guildhall, mobbed by an angry crowd who were under the impression that he had supported a clause

in the peace treaty with France which was detrimental to local trade. It was under the protection of the Mayor and his officers that the Duke was escorted to Bampfylde House. There, he was welcome and sheltered by Sir Richard Warwick Bampfylde, but the unfortunate Duke was further pursued by his assailants when he left Bampfylde House for the Castle, and again later, on his way to the Cathedral; he found peace at last when, secretly, he was able to reach the Bishop's Palace!

Sources:
Journal of the Royal Archaeological Institute, Vol 31 (paper, in 1874, by Robert Dymond)
Express & Echo, December 1933
James Crocker (1886), *Sketches of Old Exeter*
Express & Echo, November 1934
Reports in: *Express & Echo*, August 1935
The Devon & Exeter Gazette, March 192
The Times, January 1934
The *Western Morning News*, October 1929
Besley's Directories

CHAPTER 29

A High Street House (once No. 226)

What seems to be a twin-gabled, sixteenth-century house, next-door to the C&A brick-pile structure in High Street, is now a mere façade. However, we are lucky to have this shallow edifice as well as its seventeenth-century companion beside it. The two buildings, which is what they were then, were threatened with complete destruction by the local authority in the late 1950s and early '60s. This was during its period of obsessive desire to widen thoroughfares, which eventually led to one of desperate regret and the wish to narrow them.

The twin-gabled sixteenth-century house, according to Professor W.G. Hoskins, was erected in 1567 by Thomas Prestwood, a wealthy merchant of Exeter, and John Hooker, Chamberlain of Exeter considered it one of the 'good ornaments to beautify the city'. The Thomas Prestwood to whom the erection of this house is attributed, must be the man of the same name who made his will on 13 December 1576 and left money to the city's corporation of merchants for the provision of almshouses or of an annuity for the relief of four poor people who would be chosen by the Mayor. Prestwood had himself been elected Mayor in 1576, but died during his term of office.

It has also been said that another rich merchant, Simon Snow, lived in that same house. He was Mayor in 1653, and represented the city some time during the Commonwealth. Simon Snow was one of the contributors to the Hugh Crossing foundation which used the rebuilt ancient Hospital of St John* to house its institution dedicated to 'the relief and pious education of poor children.' There eventually, two schools were started. Simon Snow's gift was used to finish the school building; to build a house for the master of the Grammar School (later Exeter School); and to educate one poor boy. He also left much of his property to the city for other good causes including four scholarships to Exeter College, Oxford, for some of the deserving children. But one wonders where else in the city he had also lived, since a petition sent from Exeter to the House of Lords in 1660 records that among the materials taken from the Cathedral in Cromwell's time, was 'a great quantity of timber taken by Mr Simon Snow to be used in building and ceiling his new house.' This could hardly refer to the house that Thomas Prestwood had built in 1567!

That house, where the two eminent merchants had lived in the sixteenth and seventeenth centuries, after passing into the hands of obscure owners, became in 1781, and until his death there in 1802, the

home and place of work of another locally famous man: Robert Trewman, printer, bookseller, and founder of *Trewman's Exeter Flying Post*. That newspaper continued to be printed at this High Street house for 81 years. But the printing of other newspapers went on there until 1958. So this building's connection with printing lasted 177 years.

Robert Trewman and his associate W. Andrews, launched the first issue of their four-page, small format newspaper on 2 September 1763, from premises in South Street where the Mitre Tavern had been. It was called the *Exeter Mercury or West Country Advertiser*. A year later, they were moving to other premises in Waterbeer Street, whose address in their advertisements appeared simply as 'Behind the Guildhall'. During its publication in Waterbeer Street, the newspaper changed its name twice before acquiring its fourth and final one of *Trewman's Exeter Flying Post* in 1770. By then the partnership had been dissolved and Robert Trewman was on his own. He was 32.

In 1781 he bought the High Street house which became his home. There too, not only was the *Flying Post* printed, but Trewman also carried out business as general printer and bookseller. In fact, this place, whose only address was given as 'In High Street nearly opposite St Martin's Lane' (there was no Queen Street then) soon became a kind of centre for the intelligentsia of Exeter and the county of Devon.

The Ancient History and Description of Exeter was edited by Trewman, having been 'compiled and digested from the works of Hooker, Izacke and others', and was printed by his firm. On a visit to Exeter in 1789, King George III was presented with a copy of the book by the Dean of the Cathedral. And when the writer Isaac Disraeli (father of the Victorian statesman) visited Exeter in 1795, one of his essays was also printed at Trewman's High Street works.

Robert Trewman died at his High Street home on 20 February 1802. His obituary notice records that 'his character from his earliest age to the last moment of his life was that of the most unimpeached honour and integrity.'

Robert Trewman's widow, Mary, and son Robert, the eldest of their 13 children, continued to run the firm as partners. But Mrs Trewman survived her son by one year, Robert Trewman junr having died in 1816 at the age of 49. Father, mother and son were buried in the family vault in Bartholomew's Burial Yard (now a public garden in Bartholomew Street).

Robert Trewman the younger was succeeded by

* On a High Street site approximately opposite Boots, the chemists.

No. 226 High Street (Old Express & Echo premises until 1958). The first and second floors are the well restored but original sixteenth-century features.

The drawing was first reproduced in a newspaper (Express & Echo) on 27 November 1959 when this building was threatened with demolition.
(BY KIND PERMISSION OF FREDERICK H. BEAMISS)

one of his 12 children, Robert John, who did not, however edit the newspaper although he remained its proprietor until his death without issue in 1860. His younger brother George Robert continued to own the High Street house until he sold it in 1886 to the Devon Weekly Times and Evening Express Co. Ltd which had had a lease of the property and carried out business there since 1872. But the last copies of *Trewman's Exeter Flying Post* to be printed at the High Street works had been those of 26 March 1862. After that date the *Flying Post* was published and printed in Little Queen Street (but moved premises again before ceasing publication in 1917).

The *Devon Evening Express* which was being published and printed on the High Street premises, and the *Western Echo*, a newspaper which had been produced in Fore Street, were amalgamated under the direction of Mr James G. Owen (later Sir James) and became *The Express & Echo*. It first appeared on 1 October 1904 and its offices and works (Western Times Co.) remained in the High Street building until 1958 when they were transferred to their present premises in Sidwell Street.

In about 1828 there was only one shop (Laskey's) on the ground floor of Trewman's *Flying Post* premises, and there was still a bookselling business there. By the mid-1890s, when the *Devon Weekly Times* and *Evening Express* were published there, there were also two shops: Knowling's and Symons's.

It is impossible to say when some of the most interesting original features of the building's splendid façade became concealed behind coats of paint and plaster, but possibly this process began when Robert Trewman acquired the property in 1781.

Fortunately, in 1907 the restoration of the frontage was entrusted to Wescott, Austin & White, Exeter builders, by Sir James Owen, the proprietor of the Western Times Co., the actual work being carried out mostly by James White, one of the partners in the building firm.

The timbering of the two upper floors, which is not part of a structural frame but an externally added imitation, had been done by some other firm and displeased Sir James. This is why at this stage he commissioned Wescott, Austin & White to take over

the work of restoration.

Every timber which had to be temporarily taken down, was carefully numbered and replaced exactly where it had been originally. For the parts which had to be replaced, old oak taken from within the building was used.

In the course of the restoration, many coats of paint were removed from the woodwork of the bay-windowed first and second floors. Also lath and plaster was removed from below the windows, exposing between the carved consoles, admirable sixteenth-century panels decorated with typical arabesque designs. Originally, the arrangement was identical below the first-floor and second-floor bay-windows. But in 1907, in order to allow the insertion of the upper part of the new ground floor front, above the three doorways, the height of the timbers and arabesque panels below the first-floor bay windows, as we can still see, was reduced by half, and the arabesques had to be renewed.

Now this 1907 ground floor front has been demolished, but the first and second floors retain much of their original sixteenth-century work. And in spite of the early-twentiethth-century faked timber-frame appearance of the two upper floors, and the 1970s covered walk which replaces the ground floor, this whole façade, and its seventeenth-century companion next door, remain, in the words of John Hooker, 'good ornaments to beautify the city'.

Sources
Deeds relating to the Trewmans's property (Record Office)
The Ancient History and Description of Exeter (compiled from the works of Hooker, Izacke and others. Edited by Andrews and Trewman, first published 1765)
Trewman's Exeter Flying Post, 25 February 1802, 1 February 1816.
Biographies of Exonians, collected by George Oliver. Western Antiquary (Edited by W.H.K. Wright 1885–87)
Express & Echo, article, 27 December 1957.
Express & Echo, letters from Mr A.W. Everett (9 January 1958), Professor W.G. Hoskins (10 December 1959), Mr William T. White (23 December 1959).

CHAPTER 30

No. 227 High Street

We must be thankful that although the original interior of this High Street house has been removed, at least its attractive seventeenth-century façade remains. Its gable, slate work, round-headed window surmounted by a pediment, and the balustrades of its galleries recall the front of the Mansfield building (No. 38 North Street) which was demolished in 1972. An added interest of such façades is that with classical details, and yet, still, a general medieval appearance, they are good examples of a transitional period in architecture.

The High Street house, which dates approximately from 1660–70, underwent a careful restoration in 1878 under the supervision of Dartmouth architect, T. Lidstone. It was owned then by Messrs J.&G. Ross, and the same firm remained there until the early 1950s. Lidstone removed previous clumsy additions to the building; retained and repaired what was original; and used colour as it would have been done two centuries earlier, and only where traces of the original work showed it had been present. The restoration of the slate and plaster work was particularly successful. The *Exeter Flying Post* stated at the time that this was the first restoration in domestic architecture that had been done in Exeter, and it warmly praised the firm for its initiative.

This High Street house would have originally been built as a merchant's house, but by 1733 the City Chamber had taken a lease and was renting it for £26 a year. Some 30 years later the Chamber bought it for £600. It was used as the Judges' Lodgings (providing judges with lodgings was the joint duty of the City Corporation and the County) and the sum of £200 was agreed upon by the Corporation to furnish the house. It was known as the Mayoralty House since it was used by the Mayor and for various public functions as well as being the Judges' Lodgings during the Assizes. This lasted until 1815, at that date the City Chamber sold the house.

We are lucky to have its façade still, for in the late 1950s and early 1960s this building and its older companion, No. 226, were threatened with complete demolition. They were saved indirectly when it became unfashionable to force dual carriageways through cities, and that part of High Street was consequently allowed to retain its pre-war width.

This text is based on a detailed account of the nineteenth-century restoration of the building in the *Flying Post* of 25 September 1878, and documents in Exeter Archives.

The façade of No. 227 High Street in 1979. Dating rom c.1665, it was carefully restored in 1878.

The High Street, c.1890, showing No. 227 High Street.

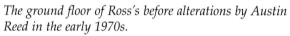

The ground floor of Ross's before alterations by Austin Reed in the early 1970s.

High Street in the early 1980s.

The two outer buildings (Boot's and Timothy White's) were demolished and replaced by others.

✦ CHAPTER 31 ✦

Deller's

Anyone who lived in Exeter then, and who was at least old enough to be taken out to tea as a special treat, would remember the famous and fabulous café-restaurant, Deller's, at the corner of Bedford Street and High Street. It was badly damaged in the air-raid of May 1942, and soon after, completely destroyed as a result of official policy.

An enthusiastic patron wrote about the place in pre-war days. 'There, one meets all one's friends and acquaintances at one time or another, taking morning coffee or afternoon tea, or lunching, dining, or supping in its bright galleries or spacious ballroom café.' At Deller's, balls, tea and dinner dances, children's parties, and even whist-drives were held, and the point was made at the time that 'the best "curtain-raiser" is to dine at Deller's before the show'.

Deller's had several rooms which served diverse occasions, one of them with its parquet floor and elaborate plaster ceiling was impressive enough for important luncheon or dinner parties to be held in it. There was also the 'Bedford Room', a public lounge, and a marvellous ball-room with a sprung floor, all designed to prompt feelings of ease and well-being. But the glory of the place was its very unusual main feature: a large volume of space whose centre between floor and roof was three-storey high without interruption, and surrounded at first and second-floor levels, by galleries rather like those which comprise the boxes in a theatre.

The capitals of the pillars which supported these galleries on two levels, the outer face of the galleries, and the walls, were all decorated with the figures in relief of adults and children involved in various scenes. As tables were laid on the centre's floor, as well as all round the first and second-floor galleries, wherever one dined, one had a interesting view of almost anything that went on, up, down, or across this fascinating architectural structure.

The architects of this building are said to have been Hyams and Hobgen of Paignton; Deller's, as a firm, certainly originated in Paignton. Edwin Deller was a painter, glazier, plumber and grocer in mid-nineteenth century Paignton, and Deller's Ltd. was established in 1844. The name persisted, and later the Paignton café area was developed by four men. One of them was an architect; another was William Lambshead, who, in about 1906, as chairman of the company, opened the first Deller's café in Exeter.

This was in a building at the corner of Martin's Lane and the Cathedral Yard, which had been until very early in this century the premises of the Exeter Bank, and which became later and extension of Clarence Hotel.

A few years after Deller's was established in Exeter, Mr and Mrs William Lambshead, who managed it, felt the premises were a little cramped considering their popularity. And so, after about ten years in the Cathedral Yard, Deller's moved to its new premises in Bedford Street.

At the corner of Bedford Street and High Street had stood an old coaching inn which, by 1890, was known as the Half Moon Hotel. It was then 'held in high estimation', the place having lately been 'thoroughly renovated' and 'at great expense... furnished and equipped... in the most comfortable and convenient manner.' It was lighted by electricity, and there were coffee-rooms, smoking-rooms, bathrooms and billiard rooms as well as all the accommodation expected of any hotel even then. The wines and spirits were 'of the best, being obtained from the most reputable sources.'

Following the Exeter tradition, it was completely demolished, and in 1912 the local architect Archibald Lucas erected on the site a one-storey building for Lloyds Bank.

Later, the new Deller's was cunningly built by its architects along High Street and Bedford Street above the bank, and beyond it they used the site from ground-floor level as far as Catherine Street. Near Catherine Street was the main entrance, whose arched doorway was flanked by decorated columns supporting an entablature on which sat and reclined female figures under a large scrolled pediment. Nearer the bank was a more modest entrance whose doorway had a straight porch held by stone brackets.

During the air raid, the building had received no direct hit; flaming debris set fire to it. The fire brigade could not cope with so much happening at the same time, and the fire-watchers on duty were neither numerous enough nor sufficiently well equipped to deal promptly with the fire. Nevertheless, as our photographs show, in spite of roof and floors having collapsed, there was enough left of this gabled brick building, with its stone-dressed, mullioned, transomed windows and decorative features, to warrant preservation and rebuilding.

When in 1916 the Bedford Street premises opened, they were not quite completed. But some difficulties due to wartime conditions resulted in the decision to leave the Cathedral Yard building on 2 December, which was a Saturday; to work the whole of the Monday on the new premises; and to open them the

This Hotel stood on the corner of High Street and Bedford Street. It was demolished to make room for Lloyds Bank in 1912.

Guests arriving at the Half Moon Hotel in the early-twentieth century.

The famous 'theatrical' galleries of Deller's where visitors could enjoy the music of a light orchestra and an atmosphere of ease and well being.

AT DELLER'S—March 1st, 1921 to January 1st, 1938

*Mr. & Mrs. L. H. Williams wish you all
a Happy and Prosperous New Year*

The dining hall of Deller's showing the elaborate plaster ceiling.

Another dining-room of Deller's.

Fancy dress ball at Deller's.

Substantial remains of Deller's after the air raid of 1942.

The 1950s structure which replaced Deller's Café.

following day. A temporary kitchen was set up; the ballroom was used for the time being as a café section; and the sale of cake took place in the lobby of the principal entrance. The main building had still a gang of men working on it; the lifts had not been installed; and tables could not be reserved. An apology to prospective customers appeared in the local newspaper.

Nevertheless, with the oak panelling not in place, the walls being covered with hessian instead, and the floor with mats, the special opening for soldiers at Deller's new Bedford Street premises went off without a hitch on Tuesday 5 of December 1916.

Deller's in Bedford Street, whose existence lasted just over a quarter of a century, probably had its most flourishing period in the 1920s and early '30s. In 1920 Mr and Mrs L.H. Williams took over the management from the Lambsheads, and in 1923, to meet the demand for extra accommodation 'created by the extreme popularity of the Bedford Street café', other premises were opened at Nos 48 and 49 High Street. But as a contemporary observer put it, 'If we want colour and music with our meals we seek them at Bedford Street, where friezes or artistic figures glowing with life, in orange, green, mauve and blue, and gilded draperies, look down on the prettily appointed tables, and an orchestra plays.'

At Bedford Street, there were bakehouses and kitchens with the best and most modern machines for almost everying, 'including pulping and straining the tomatoes for soup'. Ice creams were made on the premises and there were even dishwashing machines which were described thus 55 years ago: 'All the used plates, cups and saucers, forks, cutlery and spoons go in their separate racks, into them at one end, to pass through a veritable maelstrom of a cleansing bath, and then under big jets of boiling water, and emerge dry and shining at the other.'

In 1933 all branches of Deller's were sold to Cadena Cafés Ltd of Bristol. The café in High Street was closed in February 1964, and nowadays all that remains of the legendary Deller's is part of the name of a basement restaurant in our postwar High Street Arcade. However, in its dining-room we can see three excellent photographs of the fabulous interior of the once-famous Bedford Street establishment.

Sources:
Local Trades' Review (published 1890)
Express & Echo: December 1916, January 1917, June 1923, November 1937, October 1963, February 1964
Western Morning News: February 1933
Letters from City Librarian to enquirers: February 1964, December 1972
Deller's the Cafés of the West (published early 1920s)
Isca Collection of photographs.

✦ CHAPTER 32 ✦

London Inn Square and East Gate Site

Eastgate is the name given to the junction Sidwell Street–High Street–Paris Street–New North Road, and is a reference to what was the entrance to the city from the London, Bath and Bristol roads until 1784, when the actual East Gate was demolished. It was a massive stone structure which stood on the site which lies between the present Eastgate House and the premises of Boots the chemists.

Before the discarding of the original road pattern in the postwar reconstruction of the area, the junction of the main roads here had been far less bleak, and in pre-war days there had been a pleasant enclosure known as London Inn Square.

In those days, Southernhay East and Paris Street went their separate ways not to meet until they converged in Sidwell Street. As one emerged into that street from either of the other two, one faced houses of attractive dimensions and shapes; buildings then, lined Sidwell Street further on towards High Street than does Debenham's today. In other words, the junction of Southernhay and Paris Street

Eastgate plaque which until wartime was fixed to the wall of Mark Rowe.

Eastgate, demolished 1784.

The London Inn Square pre-war. The New London Inn was built by Matthew Nosworthy in 1794. On this site until the previous year had stood the Oxford Inn. The word 'Inn' was replaced by 'Hotel' under later management.

The original courtyard of the coaching inn converted into a hotel lounge.

The 'New London Hotel' was demolished in February 1936 to make room for a new cinema (later the ABC).

Right: The western side of London Inn Square and Northernhay Place.

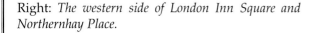

Entry in R.L.Stevenson's Handwriting in the Visitor's Book at the New London Hotel, Exeter.

Site of the Old London Inn; later replaced by The Bude Hotel & L.H. Fearis Ltd (grocers). The photo, taken after the air raid of May 1942, shows the original and separate junctions of Paris Street (left) and Southernhay (right) with Sidwell Street. The site of the damaged wall in the foreground is now part of Debenham's.

East Gate (London Inn Square) and Sidwell Street pre-war. The original premises of the Cathedral Dairy were rebuilt by the Co-operative Society in the mid 1930s.

with Sidwell Street, was not in line with New North Road: between them stood some of the Sidwell Street and Longbrook Street houses, and all this formed a much better townscape than what is there today.

London Inn Square took its name from the New London Inn, which stood until 1936 on the site of the present ABC building. Where Boots' side windows are, was the entrance to the Plaza Cinema, which had succeeded the Subscription Rooms and the Hippodrome, but retained the previous buildings' facade with its massive Ionic columns supporting an architrave. On the site of these buildings had stood, until the early part of the nineteenth century, six small almshouses with gardens, which had been founded in 1567 by William Hurst for 12 poor tradesmen of the city.

Opposite the Plaza Cinema were the houses and shops which linked Longbrook Street to Sidwell Street, the space between these shops and the Plaza being much narrower than that between Boots and Debenham's today. Facing the Savoy Cinema – as the ABC was called before, and for some time after the last war – was the Cooperative Society, which retains today the exterior of a building dating from the 1930s.

On this site, the Cathedral Dairy Co. was already

well established by 1890 and a guidebook to the Exeter trades, published at that time, states, 'From the time the milk is received till it is offered to the customer as cream or butter or junket, it is never touched by hand, and in everyway the most scrupulous purity is assured.' By 1922 the Cathedral Dairy had been absorbed by the 'Co-op', but its original building and name survived until 1936.

The New London Inn was bought by the Associated British Cinemas in May 1935, although it continued to be used as a hotel for five months. Then it was demolished in February 1936 to make room for the cinema. This was a pity, but at least nothing shameful was ever shown on the screen of 'The Savoy', and the Imperial staircase of its entrance hall, as well as its auditorium, had some dignity that the furtive corridors of the ABC, leading to its narrowly enclosed screens and Bingo placc, do not possess.

The prospect of the demolition of the eighteenth-century inn provoked anger in 1935: 'It seems incredible that anyone should be guilty of such vandalism,' wrote to the local newspaper one of the protesters. He went on, 'I write in case it should arouse others who... value our few remaining historic buildings to raise a protest against such ruthless destruction.' But

Postwar Eastgate, 1979.

such sentiments are traditionally the losers in Exeter, when there is hope of replacing an old building with some money-making structure. Although of course, the expected success of the greedy does not always materialise.

Within the angle formed by the original junction of Paris Street with Sidwell Street, once had stood the London Inn, and until September 1793, on the site of the present ABC building, was the Oxford Inn.

John Land, who had started his working life as a pig dealer and who, with hard work and thrift, had enlarged the range of his activities to include cattle in general, saved enough to become an innkeeper in Exeter. Eventually, in 1772, at the age of 42, he took over the London Inn, where he remained for some 20 years. Then, he advertised and sold it in July 1793, but stayed there until the new owner took possession of it a year later.

Meanwhile, Land had bought the Oxford Inn from its owner's widow, a Mrs Tucker, and soon after her sale by auction of all its contents in September 1793, the work of completely rebuilding the inn began. The incredible thing is that only ten months later, Matthew Nosworthy (the Exeter builder who later erected the houses of Barnfield Crescent and Dix's Field) had completed this undertaking, and John Land was able to advertise throughout July 1794, that having purchased the late Oxford Inn he had rebuilt it 'in the most commodious manner,

under the name of Land's New London Inn' and that he intended to move to it on the 31st of that month. It is described in 1806 as 'large, elegantly furnished' and as having 'every accommodation for families of the first distinction.'

The New London in John Land's days was an important coaching inn which also had a reputation for good food and wines. From the inn, according to advertisements, by 1817, every morning at 4.45 the Royal Auxiliary Fly set off for London; and only one hour later, the London Mail Coach began its journey, which took 24 hours. Daily also, was the Falmouth Mail Coach, but the Light Coach to Bristol, as well as the Light Coach to Bath, ran only six days a week. The Fly Coach to Plymouth started from the New London Inn every day at 8.45a.m., and every night at 11 o'clock the Auxiliary Fly Coach also left for Plymouth, where it arrived eight hours later. It returned from Plymouth the afternoon of the same day and was back in Exeter 24 hours after its departure from it.

Following the times of departure announced in the newspaper, was a notice which informed that the proprietors of the coaches would not be responsible for any goods damaged while being carried unless they were securely packed in proper boxes and not in wrappers, or for any goods worth more than £5 unless they had been entered as such and paid for accordingly.

John Land also advertised 'a handsome hearse and mourning coaches, with every necessary for funerals, which he will conduct in the most decent manner and on reasonable terms.'

When John Land opened his New London Inn, he was 64; when he died there on 25 January 1817, he was nearly 87. His obituary notice recorded that he was the most opulent and probably the oldest innkeeper in the West of England. It also praised his integrity and sincerity 'which marked all his transactions which rendered him highly esteemed, not only by his fellow-citizens and the principal gentry of this county, but by the first characters in the Kingdom who were in the habit of frequenting his house.'

He was buried at Pinhoe and the procession that followed his remains, as well as the crowds who lined the streets to see it, were a testimony to his wealth and popularity. The hearse which was drawn by six horses handsomely decked, and preceded by some 15 people on horseback, was followed by numerous coaches containing family and friends and post-chaises filled with coach proprietors. People had deserted all other parts of the city, and windows and house tops on the route of the procession were lined with spectators as was the road all the way to the burial place.

John Land's book-keeper succeeded his master, and after two more changes, in 1868 Robert Pople became the owner of the inn, which acquired the name of Pople's New London Hotel. Pople had the distinction of being three times Mayor of Exeter.

The New London Hotel's last owner from 1929 was W.T. Norman, the proprietor of the Bude Hotel, which was in Paris Street where the old London Inn had stood.

It has been said that at the busiest time of its coaching days, daily arrivals and departures at the New London Inn involved as many as 70 vehicles and 300 horses. Ironically, the fastest coach to cover the distance London–Exeter beat all previous records in May 1844 which was also the month and the year when the first railway (from London and Bristol) came to Exeter. The coach 'Quicksilver' had done the journey in 17 hours at an average speed of ten miles an hour.

Among the distinguished guests who stayed at the 'New London' in the course of its 142 year existence, was the Duke of Wellington in 1819, who was received enthusiastically among decoration of laurels and flowers. Other visitors of distinction included the Prince of Wales (later Edward VII), George V, Charles Dickens and Robert Louis Stevenson. It is said about the latter that in 1885, having left Bournemouth intending to go to Dartmoor, and after visiting Thomas Hardy at Dorchester on the way, he fell ill in Exeter and had to remain at the New London Hotel for several weeks. He apparently wrote in the Visitors' Book, 'Should it be your misfortune to fall sick at an inn, pray Heaven that it may be the New London.'

The New London Inn was a quadrangular building enclosing an open, cobbled yard, surrounded by a covered walk formed by pillars supporting an upper floor. Presumably this courtyard could have been reached from the back of the edifice, large doors giving carriages access to it, and the stables would also have been at the back of the inn. After coaching days had ended, the courtyard was roofed over with glass and minor alterations were carried out which, with the addition of furniture, a few rugs, palms, ferns, and seasonal flowers, contributed to the creation of a very attractive hotel lounge where it was a pleasure to sit, and which remained virtually unchanged until the destruction of the building in 1936 by the cinema company.

The exterior of the 'New London' was typically Georgian. The ground-floor windows were round-headed and the other sash windows, at first and second floor levels, were rectangular, comprising 12 panes. The entrance porch was of the Doric order, four fluted columns supporting an entablature whose frieze had plain metopes between the triglyphs.

London Inn Square itself was an attractive enclosure and must have been an even more intimate one when the inn adjoined Longbrook Street before the cutting in 1833 of New North Road. The Square became almost as famous as the Inn itself. It was a kind of social centre for Exeter and one where speakers addressed or read to a crowd of eager listeners. Gladstone is said to have addressed a mass political meeting there at the height of his career.

After Robert Louis Stevenson's illness at the New London Hotel, a memorial pane was placed in the window of the room he had occupied. Translated from the Latin, it says, 'In this bedroom R.L.S. lay ill on 5th September, 1885. His prisonhouse, the body, was weak and fragile, but his was the bright spirit. This panel was placed here by two admirers of his books which are, in very truth, a more enduring monument.' Although the Exeter museum still has three decorated panes which are said to have come from the memorial window, and which were donated in 1936 by the Associated British Cinemas, the pane that bears the inscription cannot be traced.

Sources
Trewman's Exeter Flying Post, July and September 1793; July and August 1794; January and February 1817
A. Jenkins (1806), *History and Description of the City of Exeter*
R. Dymond (1880), *Old Inns and Taverns of Exeter*
Express & Echo articles, July 1958, July 1966
Express & Echo letter from reader, September 1935
Western Morning News letters from readers, April 1935, May 1950)
Isca Collection of photographs

✦ CHAPTER 33 ✦

The Rougemont Site

Not far from where stood the London Inn are Rougemont House and Garden. It took William the Conqueror 18 days of siege to break the resistance of the people of Exeter in 1068. So not quite trusting them afterwards, the Normans looked for a suitable site on which to build a castle as a possible defence against the citizens themselves. Rougemont Hill was chosen.

Just within Rougemont Garden, as we enter it from Castle Street, we can see the remains of this castle's massive gate-house. The pointed arches with straight sides, of such early Norman work, sometimes mislead people into thinking that they belong to the Saxon period.

The curving northern section of the ancient city wall was used by the Normans as part of their castle wall, and they built a new wall to join the old one and

form with it an enclosure (now Castle Yard). In Rougemont Garden, although we are within the city wall, we see the outer side of the Norman wall, and below it, what was the earth bank and the moat of the castle. All this was part of the inner ward; further away, and concentrically, was the outer ward, still represented by the deep slope in front of the old university building in Gandy Street. The outer ward would have stretched in a semi-circle to the site of Boots and joined the city wall there.

Besieged in 1136 by King Stephen's army for three months before its occupiers, the Earl of Devon and his men, surrendered, it was not however until the Prayer Book Rebellion some 400 years later that Rougemont Castle suffered greatly in the course of a siege by the Rebels, and soon fell into decay. After its use as a strong point by the Royalists in the Civil War,

Aerial view showing Rougemont House in the foreground and the 1774 building in Castle Yard.

The above picture is a reproduction of a water-colour drawing of buildings existing in the area of the Castle of Exeter before the erection of the first Sessions House in 1618. The latter was replaced in 1774 by the present building.

Early Norman gate to Rougemont Castle.

Above and above right: *Built in Castle Yard in 1774. Here the Assizes and Quarter Sessions were held, and later the Crown Courts.*

Castle Street leading to Castle Yard.

Portrait of John Patch, born 1723, died 1787.

Rougemont House, built 1770 by John Patch but much altered in the early-nineteenth century by Edmund Granger.

Rougemont House, acquired by the City, was opened to the public on 2 April 1912.

the Castle was dismantled and most of its towers were destroyed. All that remains, and which includes a bastion misleadingly known as Athelstan Tower, is built of the volcanic stone quarried nearby and called Northernhay stone.

Rougemont Castle, which had been in the custody of the Earls of Devon, became in 1232, by a decision of Henry III, the property of the Earls of Cornwall who owned that county. But when some 100 years later Edward III promoted his son Edward from Earl to Duke of Cornwall and so raised the status of the county to that of duchy, the Castle became part of the Duchy of Cornwall.

By permission of the Dukes of Cornwall, the Assizes and Quarter Sessions were held within the Castle, and later, in a seventeenth-century building which was replaced in 1774 by the present one where the Crown Courts are now held.

In 1819, the Castle and the adjoining site became the property of the County of Devon. However, an annual payment of £10 to the Duchy of Cornwall went on being paid by the County throughout the period of its ownership of the Castle, and the liability for this payment passed to the Secretary of State for the Environment under a deed of 18 April 1978 which conveyed the Castle from the County to the State.

Rougemont Gardens in the early 1980s.

This payment has its origin in an Act of Parliament of 1773 allowing the demolition by the Duchy of the seventeenth-century Shire Hall within the Castle precincts, and the building of a new Shire Hall for the County 'in a more commodious manner'. Thus there is still a connection between Exeter Castle and the Duchy of Cornwall!

The site of Rougemont Garden, once the glacis and moat of the Castle, and by 1768 in appalling condition, was rented then from the Duchy of Cornwall by John Patch. Although a medical man by profession, he had a passion for gardening. Much in this garden, as we see it today, we owe to John Patch. He laid out the grounds, making the most of the unevenness of the land, and planted a variety of fine trees. So what had been referred to as 'a neglected and disgusting hole', became under his direction 'a paradise in miniature'. Then in about 1770 he built Rougemont House in the north-east corner of the site.

John Patch, who in 1741 at the age of 18 was elected one of the first five surgeons of the new Devon and Exeter Hospital, had been educated at Exeter (Grammar) School, and had studied anatomy, surgery and mathematics at Edinburgh. He

returned to Exeter after his marriage, and when his father, also a doctor, died he took over his practice. He was then 23.

John Patch, according to one of his contemporaries, seems to have combined exceptional qualities, being appreciated for his warmth and kindness as well as admired for his soundness of judgement and his encyclopaedic knowledge.

A print of 1794 in Exeter Library shows Rougemont House as the Georgian house that Patch had built some 20 years earlier. How different it looks from the Regency building it became and which we see today! The original house was a square brick building; the front of it faced Castle Street, and instead of a high wall, there was a little lawn between the house and the street. What in the present building is a first floor on the Castle Street side was the ground floor in the eighteenth century.

The house had then a typically Georgian entrance and porch. The doorway was level with the street, but it has become a first-floor window and the original basement is now, on this side, the ground floor.

After the death of John Patch in 1787, Edmund Granger, a wool merchant who had a house and mills in Exwick, rented Rougemont House and grounds,

*The War Memorial erected
after the First World War.*

but in 1798 he was able to buy the property freehold from the Duchy of Cornwall. It was he who had the house enlarged and its appearance greatly altered.

When the house was converted, in the early-nineteenth century, some excavations took place down to the level of the kitchen and servants' quarters. This necessitated building a retaining wall along Castle Street. The window openings on the present second and third floors are the original ones, but they belonged once respectively to the first and second floors. The windows of the upper storey, according to Georgian fashion, are smaller than those of lower floors. This can also be seen on the Rougemont Garden side of the house.

On this side, the twin curves of the ground floor, which protrude from the rest of the house and contain the windows, are Regency-style additions. So are the verandah and the high first-floor windows, the external curved walls, and the stucco over the whole building, which conceals the brickwork of the eighteenth-century house that John Patch built.

Rougemont House and its grounds were privately owned until they were acquired by the city in 1911. The city wall, forming the boundary to the grounds on the west side, was then pierced to make a doorway giving access to and from Northernhay Gardens. Rougemont Garden was opened to the public on 2 April 1912.

Apart from the black-and-white-tiled floor and the staircase in the hall, which are the original eighteenth-century features, the interior of Rougemont House has been somewhat altered, being adapted to its present function. It is one of Exeter's little museums.

Sources
George Oliver, *History of the Castle*
Transactions of the Devonshire Association
Deeds in Record Office relating to John Patch and Edmund Granger re Rougemont House and grounds
Plan of the Castle Precinct by Norden (1617)
Documents in Record Office relating to Castle Site
Deed of 18 April 1978 in the County Secretary's Dept at County Hall, Exeter

Sidwell Street in its tram days.

The junction of New North Road and Longbrook Street, pre-war.

A house in Poltimore Square. Also showing a cottage in Warren Lane, now demolished. (J.W.)

CHAPTER 34

Within Sidwell Street, Longbrook Street and Warren Lane

Named after the brook which is piped until it meets the river at the end of Exe Street, Longbrook Street now begins beside the massive Debenham store, at a barren, windy junction, on the site of which shops and houses stood until 1942.

A little way down Longbrook Street, leading to the multi-storey car park, we find on our right a new road called King William Street. Whether this refers to the Conqueror, his son, or one of the other two kings of England of the same name, is not clear, but that none of them could have felt flattered by being recalled here is certain. As we look up that street, we see six levels of concrete planks forming the car park; a plain, grey-brick tower; and the gloomy backs of new buildings.

Past King William Street, mercifully (if incongruously) Hampton Place, a small terrace of three-storey early-nineteenth-century houses with dormer windows, is still there. But just beyond them, also on our right, and opposite the Black Horse Inn, is a narrow dead-end at the top of which we, again, have a view of the car park's concrete planks. Until the mid-1960s, the dead-end was a real lane leading to Poltimore Square and Terrace, and to Warren Lane. People lived there, most of the houses were structurally sound; and they, the lanes and the gradient of the land formed a delightful townscape. An old wall, some granite curbstones, and a small brick platform are what is left of the charming square and terrace.

A few yards further on in Longbrook Street, still on our right, we come to Warren Lane. On our left as we enter it, along its side, is a tarmac slope (it used to be a long and pretty garden) leading to Longbrook House; the first house of a pleasant nineteenth-

century terrace once called Park Place, which faces Longbrook Street. Warren Lane, which, oddly, still has a paved gutter on one side, until the mid-1960s had retained its tiers of eighteenth- and nineteenth-century houses, arranged in terraces following its steep slope. Higher than Park Place was Sidwell Terrace, and further up still, on the same side, the cottages of Warren Place faced the lane and the narrow way to Poltimore Square on the other side of it. All very picturesque.

The late-Georgian brick houses of Poltimore Square formed an attractive corner with Warren Lane. Further on was Poltimore Terrace, an elegant assembly of stuccoed, Regency-style houses in excellent condition, and at right-angles with them were the houses of Buller Place. All this was demolished in the late 1960s in fulfilment, it was said at the time, of a promise made to Debenham's (when the firm was still known as Bobby's), that there would be a multi-storey car park close to its ambitiously large new store. Thus, we now have a car park where, until some 12 years ago, there was an attractive, peaceful and conveniently situated residential precinct, whose houses had been officially described as 'mostly still able to command a reasonably high level value.'

Warren Lane now stops at a wasteland from which we have a full view of this car park: an oppressive mass formed by piled up strips of concrete and gloomy space. The lane continued past Sidwell Terrace and Warren Place; just before it twisted sharply to the left to join Church Lane, we now have a foot-stamped track across the wasteland. It leads to the new, wide King William Street, which has pushed

Poltimore Square, demolished to make room for a multi-storey car park in the late 1960s.

The Regency style houses in Poltimore Terrace, all demolished in the erection of the multi-storey car park.

Aerial view of the pre-war street pattern in the London Inn Square area (East Gate)

its way round the massive car park from Longbrook Street, and here has thoughtlessly absorbed the name, and recklessly stretched the width of Church Lane (which went along the church grounds from Sidwell Street to York Road).

However, if we cross the new street, we find that between it and Sidwell Street, a little of Church Lane remains, with, on our left as we walk towards Sidwell Street, the pleasingly warm colour and rough texture of the original wall, made of the coarse Heavitree sandstone and of a later addition of attractive eighteenth-century handmade bricks. Here a blocked gateway shows that there was once an entrance to the churchyard from Church Lane. Warren Lane probably was made to give easy access to St Sidwell's Church from the Longbrook Street area. It certainly was used in this way in the early-eighteenth century.

It is interesting, as we emerge into Sidwell Street (by Tesco), to cross it and to observe what has been erected on its north-western side between St Sidwell's churchyard and the converging point of Sidwell Street with Longbrook Street.

First we come to the Tesco block, which has alternating vertical strips of glass and brick, and whose first floor is supported by shafts of concrete. This is typical of the ubiquitous 'pile-and-panel' design for relatively low buildings in the 1960s. Then, we look at the Maples block. This one is also on piles, but it has no windows except for one, proportionately small, horizontal strip of glass. The necessary function within the interior of a building need not result in such drabness in its elevation. Not if architects

have imagination. Next to this mostly blank face, is an all-window block (like its neighbours, on stilts), more typical of the 1950s, when the glass-house conception for the design of buildings had become unrestrained and widespread. None of these buildings, squared off at the top, shows any roof. The right interplay between roof lines is an essential contribution to good townscape. To be unaware of this, particularly in the rebuilding of a city like Exeter, is deplorable.

Let us consider some of the buildings which were on this site (still, in the mid-1960s) before the erection of the present structures.

Nos. 20–24 Sidwell Street was a handsome red brick Georgian terrace with the typical stone band the whole width of the façade, keystones, a cornice and parapet, and the usual well-recessed sash windows, some of the glazing bars being original.

A delicately shaped fanlight and porch had survived, in spite of shops having been made out of the ground floors of these houses, which had originally been solely residential.

At No. 21, in the 1890s, were Messrs E. Denney & Co., the best photographers in Exeter. Their shop front, which was in 'handsome black and gold', was described at the time as 'an attractive feature of the thoroughfare'. Opal work was a speciality, delicate pictures being produced in sepia, 'Bartolozzi' red, blue, green or 'any desired tints'. Bromide pictures were growing into favour and some as enlargements were said to be particularly beautiful. 'There are few persons of note... who have not... favoured Messrs Denney.'

The construction of Debenham's store, in Sidwell Street, dominating the older buildings, which were eventually to be demolished.

The Regency façade of Nos 15–16 Sidwell Street, built c.1820, demolished in the mid-1960s. This became the site of Liptons and the Pram & Toy Shop. (J.W.)

At No. 22 were in those days, the Misses Harriet and Elizabeth Brown, stay makers. The business had been there since 1830. The object in each article made by the Misses Brown was, 'to support and improve the figure', and to achieve this, these ladies used 'a thorough knowledge of the anatomical construction of the body.' Where strength was necessary, it was said tactfully, the goods were made accordingly. The premises, described as handsome and unique, had then a wide arch above the centre of the shop window, and pilasters on either side, which were all surmounted by decorated pediments.

As for No. 20 (next door to the photographer), it was in the 1890s the residence of the surgeon Edward Steele-Perkins. (Members of this well-known family still live in Exeter and other parts of Devon.) Alfred Steele-Perkins, another medical man of the same family, was living at No. 29 Sidwell Street (this was a little nearer Church Lane). He was Mayor of Exeter in 1894–95.

On the western side of Alfred Steele-Perkins's house, and adjoining it, stood until some 90 years ago John Webb's Almshouses. He had left an endowment in 1676 for the benefit of these almshouses and their four women occupants (chosen in the course of the years by the trustees). These houses, which had been repaired in 1730, and again in 1815–25, were described earlier in the nineteenth century as 'gloomy habitations consisting of one room each with a small garden behind.' The entrance to each habitation was on the side of the building, through an archway fronting Sidwell Street, and the herb garden to which each occupant was entitled, extended at the back towards Warren Lane. These poor women received additional relief from the Charity when ill; meat at Christmas; and beer when their allowance was due every quarter. By 1825 this was £1.5s., but when the Charity had incurred the expense of having to repair the building, the allowance to each inmate had been reduced for a while by a few shillings per quarter!

Tesco is on the site of all these various houses.

A fine Regency façade formed Nos. 15–16 Sidwell Street until the mid-1960s. It was the property of Messrs Force & Sons, the estate agents, and already belonged to the Force family in 1822 (they had probably built the house not long before that date). This four-storey building, a single house originally, had a stuccoed front and a modillion cornice beneath its parapet. Its six bow windows had 32 panes each. Inside this graceful building, from its first floor, the staircase was original, the handrail curving elegantly upward surmounting slender balusters. Other interesting features were the glass cupola above the stair that gave light to it; the fanlight with delicate tracery above a landing door; and the plaster work of the ceiling in one of the front rooms. Liptons and the Pram & Toy Shop are now on this site.

Porch Place, Exon Court and Clodes Court were until 1936 between No. 75 and No. 80 Sidwell Street. By 1937 they had been demolished and the site was being prepared for the erection of the Odeon Cinema.

Right: *No. 21 Sidwell in the 1890s, premises of Denney & Co., 'the Best Photographers in Exeter'.*

Upper Sidwell Street, c.1900.

The bombed corner of Sidwell Street, which was to become the site of Debenhams.

Sidwell Street in the early 1980s.

Until the bombing of 1942, buildings lined the converging sides of Longbrook Street and Sidwell Street much further on than they do today. The shops which joined these converging sides and faced London Inn Square, at right-angles (approximately) with the Savoy Cinema (now the ABC), were quite close to that building, about as close on its eastern side as Boots is on its western side today. Also, these eastern and western sides were built further to the south than are the new structures, since High Street here was about half its present width. London Inn Square was formed by these two sides of houses and shops, and the Savoy Cinema (which had replaced the eighteenth-century inn since 1936).

The brutally straight, wide road in front of Debenham's, did not exist. Here, now, pedestrians can be exposed to icy winds while waiting for the dense traffic to allow them passage. Southernhay came out into Sidwell Street where Paris Street joins the junction today, but it was only half the width of this new Paris Street. So, in those days, coming out of Southernhay, one had to turn left towards High Street, then right at London Inn Square towards the cinema, and right again for Longbrook Street.

In postwar days, at the destruction of the street pattern, Paris Street was made to run into Southernhay; it was doubled in width; and an uncouth new road was cut to join it to New North Road.

Now, the truncated corner Longbrook Street–Sidwell Street is formed by Debenham's, whose big, flat, glass-house face looks above and beyond all other buildings nearby, and which imposes its regrettable shape and size forcefully as we walk up High Street. Cliff-like, it also catches the wind and breaks it into swirling currents of air that will penetrate anywhere within this over-spaced, pentadactyl junction.

Sources
Articles in *Express & Echo* (Jacqueline Warren, 1 December, 1960, 8 February 1965)
Where To Buy (guidebook, 1890)
Maps of Exeter (Sutton Nicholls, 1723; John Tallis, 1860)
Report of the Commissioners (concerning charities of Exeter 1825)
George Townsend (1909), *Sketches of Bygone Exeter*

The Seven Stars Inn (later 'Hotel') at the corner of Okehampton Road near Exe Bridge was the origin of Exeter's theatres.

CHAPTER 35

Exeter Theatres

On the present site of the Automobile Association in Bedford Street once stood a theatre which had been erected in 1787. This was Exeter's second theatre; it was destroyed by fire in 1820. However, the colonnade of the building's façade was spared and it was incorporated in the new theatre which was erected within a few months. Unfortunately in 1885 this theatre also collapsed in a fire. Exeter's fourth theatre was built on a new site: at the corner of Longbrook Street and New North Road. It only lasted 11 months; it was Exeter's third theatre to be lost in a fire. The city's fifth theatre was erected on the same site in 1889. A demolition squad destroyed it in 1963.

A letter from Bishop Grandisson on 9 August 1352, forbidding the performance of a play he considered disreputable and harmful, shows that Exeter possibly had a theatre in the fourteenth century. But the word 'theatrum' in this context may have referred to no more than a movable stage. Again, 200 years later, Exeter may have had a theatre.

A document in the British Museum relates that in the course of a performance of *Doctor Faustus*, the devil himself suddenly appeared beside the actor taking the part of Mephistopheles and that the panic-stricken audience fled from the house and the actors from the town.

Early newspapers show that at the beginning of the eighteenth century, plays in Exeter were performed in the large room of the Seven Stars Inn. But what can be called Exeter's first theatre with some certainty, and in our sense of the word, was in Waterbeer Street, on the site of the Old Police Station, where at present a low wall encloses a flower bed in the centre of which a statue is said to be 'Looking Forward'.

Much was made then of the fact that this theatre was only across the way from the Turk's Head. The entrance to the pit was from Goldsmith Street – the street of which only a short section has now been spared, so that it can lead from High Street to the new Guildhall Square.

The theatre, opened in Bedford Street in 1821, was destroyed by fire in 1885. Its eighteenth-century predecessor on the site had suffered the same fate. This photograph is the only known photographic record, as far as The Isca Collection is aware, of this Bedford Street Theatre. It was found by accident and its owner was not aware of what building it was.

Only 11 months after its erection on a new site the Theatre Royal was gutted by fire in September 1887.

This Waterbeer Street theatre had been built in 1749 with the help of Andrew Brice, the clever, boisterous, humorous, gossip-loving printer, whose satirical works were said to have 'exposed and reformed many ridiculous customs'. After various difficulties encountered over the first 15 years of its existence, Exeter's first theatre acquired a regular company of actors. But some 20 years later, the need was felt for grander premises, and so came into being Exeter's second theatre, the first on the Bedford Street site.

Its opening night on 10 October 1787, was a great event in Exeter. The exterior of the building was illuminated with candles, and as they moved in to find their seats, group after group broke into applause when they saw the magnificence of the interior.

Sarah Siddons in 1790, and Edmund Kean in 1811, were the nationally famous actress and actor who appeared on the stage of this Exeter theatre. But in the early hours of 8 March 1820, a fire was started by a gas-lit chandelier which was so close to the rafters

that the heat caused the roof to burst into flame. The theatre was comply destroyed except for its colonnade outside, which remained to form the front of a new theatre that was opened in 1821, but on 7 February 1885, it was also destroyed by fire. Curiously, the Drill Hall, on the same site, had the same tragic end in one of the air raids of May 1942.

Even more tragic was the end of Exeter's fourth theatre on 5 September 1887, 11 months after its opening on the new site. Towards the end of a performance of the play *Romany Rye*, tinted gauzes used for lighting effects were blown onto naked gas jets causing sparks and flames to appear on the stage. The fire spread rapidly. People were trapped and died of suffocation; some were trampled to death; others were killed by throwing themselves into the street from high balconies; 200 perished.

This disaster led to the complete revision of the safety regulations for places of entertainment throughout the country. When the Theatre Royal was

The Theatre Royal Fire of 1887

Interior of the theatre.

The destruction by fire of the Theatre Royal.

Finding the remains of bodies in the ruins.

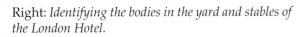

Right: Identifying the bodies in the yard and stables of the London Hotel.

The bulging of the curtain at the beginning of the fire.

Fire engine.

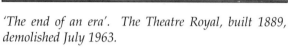

'The end of an era'. The Theatre Royal, built 1889, demolished July 1963.

Interior of the Theatre Royal in Longbrook Street.

(J.W.)

The Theatre Royal standing at the junction of Longbrook Street and New North Road.

The replacement for the Theatre Royal, 1979.

rebuilt in 1889, it had the first of a new type of safety curtain, and it was lighted by electricity; the stage had 358 lights of 16 candlepower each. The *Yeoman of the Guard* was its first performance on 7 October 1889.

During the 74 years of its existence, the Theatre Royal was visited by several well-known actors and actresses and by excellent repertory companies, but the most famous actor to appear on its stage was Sir Henry Irving in 1905.

To those who had known the visual splendour of this theatre's pantomimes and remembered the line of coaches along Longbrook Street, awaiting every night the end of the performance to return people to their towns and villages; to those who had witnessed the popularity of plays performed by such as the Malvern Company, and the success of amateur productions by the Operatic Society or Mrs Gamble's chosen few; to those for whom the Theatre Royal was also a meeting-place where one could recognise among the large and glittering audience many familiar faces, it was a shock when, through lack of support for the live theatre, some time after the last war, it was turned into a cinema.

The attempt to revert to live theatre in 1959, and the use of the place, on occasion, as a concert hall, were not successful, and although it was reprieved for a year in 1960, the decision to demolish the building was eventually taken; it was dismembered in July 1963.

Exeter now has a good little theatre perched on a university hill difficult of access for those who have not the use of a car, and for all on nights of severe frost or heavy snow falls.

Sources

Transactions of the Devonshire Association
Contemporary reports in *Exeter Flying Post* and *Express & Echo*

Clapperbrook Lane, now with the sprawl of the Marsh Barton Industrial Estate.

Ide Lane once joined Alphington to Ide. It is seen here (right) cut off by a link road to the A30.

CHAPTER 36

Lost Rural Aspects

The beginning of Clapperbrook Lane at Alphington.

Left: A few years ago the rural Clapperbrook Lane continued past the gate.

A rural aspect which existed until the 1960s very close to some parts of the city, is an amenity that has been lost by Exeter. A good example of this loss is Clapperbrook Lane, which ran from the west bank of the canal at Salmon Pool Bridge, to Alphington very near the church.

It was a delightful, leafy country lane which climbed up and down a narrow humped bridge under whose stones flowed the ungirded Alphin Brook. The lane went on across peaceful meadows before it reached some picturesque cottages on its Alphington side.

To those who, until a few years ago, were able to enjoy this country walk so near an urban area, it remains a shock, after crossing the canal and railway bridges, to see the municipal refuse incinerator with its tall chimney, and the industrial buildings of the sprawling grid of the Marsh Barton estate, where the tree-lined lane had meandered diagonally over a brook and across fields. It is a shock, too, to come to the end of the remaining short length of Clapperbrook Lane from its Alphington side, and to face the same industrial estate, from the opposite direction, with the concrete trench of the imprisoned brook in the foreground.

Clapperbrook Lane was part of an ancient way which would have made it possible, hundreds of years ago, for travellers coming from the London road and going to Plymouth, to by-pass the walled city of Exeter. At Heavitree, they could have turned south and reached a track along the line of the present Barrack Road, then continued down Salmon Pool Lane as far as the Priory of St James by the river (the site of the present Old Abbey Court flats). Nearby, was the ford called Madford, which was a point at which the river could be crossed. A track from its western side led directly to Clapperbrook Lane before the canal was built, and thus travellers could have reached Alphington Church and the Plymouth road.

Two other lanes which, until recently, could be enjoyed for country walks by city people, were Ide Lane and Stone Lane. The enchanting Ide Lane which, between hills, followed the Alphin meadows, joined Alphington, near its church, to Ide's Fore Street. This lane has been absorbed by the new section of the A30.

Stone Lane, with its hedgerow, wild flowers, and stile, was a short but delightful bit of countryside between Alphington Road and Cowick Lane. It has been obliterated by a new estate to the north of St Thomas's Girls' School.

The centre of Countess Wear Village, c.1940.

Countess Wear House, built in 1714, is a good example of Queen Anne architecture.

✦ CHAPTER 37 ✦

Countess Wear

Countess Wear, south-east of Exeter, is an attractive area within walking distance from the city, which has, however, lost some of its rural charm during the last 20 years.

What has been lost is open space covered with orchards and large cultivated gardens, a fine barn, other functional and attractively textured stone buildings, and colourful old walls. All these were mostly between Countess Wear Road and Mill Road. Still, new houses built within that space might have had shapes and colour schemes which blended happily with the original white-washed, thatch-roofed cottages of the village. But many houses which have been erected on this site are not suited to their environment.

If we walk down School Lane and turn left into Mill Road, it is a pleasure to see that the delightful early-Georgian little red-brick house called The Barton is still there, but facing it, the new pseudo-Georgian-cum-Regency terrace, built on the land which surrounded the mill, is hardly an improvement to the district.

On the same side as The Barton, a little further on, part of the old wall, pleasingly adorned with hanging greenery, has been demolished. Here the steep land has been levelled, and a straight line of semi-detached brick houses now stands there without any regard for the character of the area.

On the mill leat side, Withymead has a fine garden, and its modern extension, slate-hung, is a rare example of befitting contemporary architecture in Countess Wear.

The steep, narrow path which starts between Millstone Cottage and a gabled house in Mill Road has retained much of its charm, with flowering bushes, trees and old stone and brick walls on either side. Here a new well-paved forecourt is an attractive feature, but on the other side of this footpath, at a higher level, several new houses, particularly the grey-brick one which replaces a fine old barn, seem to have been built with little thought for this environment of original cottages and splendid scenery. But at the top of the path, two attractively tiled and curving old walls partly enclose new gardens which have delightful views of the river and hills.

A little further on in Mill Road, the gable, bay-window, balcony and colour scheme of a house called Reylands, succeed in making this small building fit nicely into the original surroundings.

If we walk on along Mill Road, we come to the unmade part of this lane whose dust and stone surface is straight out of the past. No building has so far spoilt the green strip between leat and lane. But the lime kilns are almost completely covered with weed and overgrown bushes, which give this spot a derelict aspect. Yet it could be tidied up, with the old kilns becoming an interesting part of this country lane. A little further on still, stand the original, white-washed, thatch-roofed cottages of Countess Wear. A disappointment here is a new house whose over-gabled shape, and colour, are regrettable, particularly, close as it is to the original cottages. Yet, next to it, a newer house, with a normally sized gable, white walls, and brown paint, fits in very successfully next to these cottages.

Hillside, in a little street which joins Countess Wear Road to Mill Lane, has tiny windows and a small porch. It is one of the delightful, thatched cottages of this narrow and picturesquely curving way, at the top of which, unfortunately, have been built houses of unbecoming design. Mercifully, Mill Thatch still overlooks Mill Lane, and next to it, Exe View, whose mop of thatch slopes down to its eaves like a thick fringe, is still part of an enchanting scene as one walks towards the dip of Countess Wear Road.

The village street which joins Countess Wear Road to Mill Lane.

Countess Wear village, c.1930.

Countess Wear village, 1979.

The Old Glass House in Glasshouse Lane

The gardens of the Old Glass House stretching towards the river.

In Countess Wear Road, from the attractive riverside green where a defunct Town Clerk still orders 'Do not paddle or bathe here', a most effective view of the cottages is somewhat spoilt by the soaring point of a new and unfitting house.

Not so long ago, facing this green, was a group of thatched cottages which, with others, formed a beautifully rural picture, particularly when seen from the higher ground next to the retaining wall of the playing-fields. These cottages, in the dip of Countess Wear Road, have unfortunately been replaced by houses not suited to this particular site.

From their terraces, however, there is a fine view of the river and the hills. The Exe here flows in an almost straight course towards the road before turning right on its way to the bridge. Beyond the river and the meadows are the hills of Haldon, but nearby, across the meeting-place of the leat and the main stream, surrounded by water, is 'Scotland'. This is the name of that small island according to an eighteenth-century map of Devon.

If we walk on along Countess Wear Road towards Bridge Road, we come to Countess Wear House, a very fine red-brick building which dates from 1714 and is a good example of Queen Anne architecture. It was used in that century as a French hospital. The Huguenot colony in Exeter had apparently its own hospital near the city, as well as its own church in the city itself.

The bridge over the river at Countess Wear was erected in 1760 and was originally narrow. Until

Countess Wear Bridge, 1980.

then, the river there had to be crossed by a ford. In 1772 one of the piers fell in and when two years later new piers were built and the bridge was reopened, tolls were collected. The stage-coach on weekdays was charged 2s.6d., and an extra charge of 1s. was made if there were more than six passengers inside! Tolls were paid at the toll-house which later became known as the Redbrick Cottage. It was demolished some 15 years ago when the road was widened.

If we cross Bridge Road from Countess Wear Road, we reach Glass House Lane. It follows the river and has mostly retained its rural aspect until it reaches a modern estate and turns sharp left towards Topsham Road.

At this point is a group of picturesque thatch-roofed cottages and here also remains, in its secluded garden, the Old Glass House. Externally this thatched house seems to date from the early-eighteenth century, but it apparently incorporates parts which are much older. Glass was made here until 1690. When digging was taking place in the making of a drive to the garage, some 30 years ago, a large circular work of masonry, rather like a well but larger, was discovered. The then owner wondered whether this had had some connection with the manufacturing of glass.

The village of Countess Wear owes its name to the famous weir that stopped the river being navigable to Exeter and which was first built by Isabella Countess of Devon in 1284, and then irretrievably consolidated 27 years later by her successor Hugh Courtenay. The remains of this weir can still be seen under the water above Countess Wear Bridge.

Sources

Transactions of the Devonshire Association
Map book of the Chamber of Exeter, c.1770–85
Map of the County of Devon (Benjamin Donn, 1765)

✦ CHAPTER 38 ✦

Bowhill

The fact that once there were two Bowhills in Dunsford Hill – then known as Moreton Road – has at times been confusing. The Bowhill House that stood on the site which forms the corner of Buddle Lane and Dunsford Hill, was purchased towards the end of the eighteenth century and converted into what was then called a lunatic asylum. This was opened on 1 July 1801. Eventually, the site was used to build John Stocker School.

But further up the hill is the far more interesting house called Bowhill, whose original features are typical of the fifteenth century. It is one of the buildings which form Exeter's architectural heritage and which have from time to time been threatened with demolition. Bowhill, according to a report on ancient monuments, was threatened in 1938. But demolition was put off; then came the war; and in 1947 it was scheduled as a Grade II building by the Ministry of Town and Country Planning. Although the original appearance of the house has been somewhat changed by additions and alterations over the years, it is still a fine and interesting building.

The part of the house that can be seen from the main road, and which is parallel to it, is the south range; at either end of it is a wing, the three sides thus forming a courtyard at the back. All the outer walls of the buildings at ground-floor level, and nearly all at first-floor level, are the original fifteenth-century ones. Unfortunately, of the original windows, the south range retains only three small ones on the Dunsford Hill side; and on the Bowhay Lane side, only the surrounding stonework and mullion of what was a two-light fifteenth-century window, are left. All the dripstones remain, though, and so do the cusps of the small windows.

The west wing is formed by the original kitchen which still has its ceiling of chamfered beams and joists, and a large volcanic stone fireplace with its bread oven. As for the eastern range, the two square-headed, mullioned, transomed and cusped two-light windows, their level, the chimney-breast, and the position of the arched and moulded doorway, as seen from Bowhay Lane, all show that on the other side of this wall there must be an important room. It was in fact the banqueting-hall. The doorway gives access to what could have been the screens (a passage) at the south end of the hall.

Bowhill is not only architecturally, but also histor-

An early sketch of Bowhill before restoration.

Bowhill in the 1930s.

Bowhill House, 1979. Bowhill (c.1430), after some restoration, fell again into neglect, before being restored further.

Wood panelling in the interior of Bowhill.

Interior doorway.

Fifteenth-century fireplace and bread oven in the kitchen.

ically interesting, for it is connected with the history of the city and county. It was originally the residence of the Holland family, and was probably built for Richard Holland since its style is that of the period during part of which he was a member of Parliament for Devon (1430).

Richard's son and grandson became in turn members of Parliament for Exeter. It was through Richard's great-granddaughter, Thomasina Holland, marrying John Carew, who was Sheriff of Cornwall in 1488, that the manor of Bowhill passed into the hands of the famous Carew family.

Grace, the youngest of the three daughters of Thomas Carew, who was Recorder of Exeter in 1676, married Francis Sawle, and it was their son Richard who, in 1750, inherited the Bowhill estate, which included the nearby land of Barley. By then, Barley House had been built by his cousin John Pinnock who had left him the estate, and so Richard Sawle went to live at Barley House, as Pinnock had done. Barley House is now the administrative centre of Devon County Council Library Services.

When the two daughters of Richard Sawle inherited the estate in 1773, it had to be divided, and some 20 years later the land round the original house of Bowhill was sold. But a right of carriage entrance, along the line of Bowhay Lane, was reserved to keep access open to Barley House from the Moreton Road.

The gardens of Bowhill had been used as nurseries for a considerable time when the house was sold in 1968. It was then restored and opened as a restaurant which lasted for a few years. The house is now (February 1978) shut up for repair, and under the supervision of the Department of the Environment.

The interior retains very fine original features. The banqueting-hall has a handsome arch-braced roof with windbraces between the wall-plate and the lower purlins, and the coving above the arch-braces is formed by collar-braces supported by the upper level of purlins.

At the east end of the south range, fronting the main road, is a room whose ceiling is formed by moulded beams which cross one another. The room above has a beautiful arch-braced roof with several carved bosses. Also on the first floor, but at the west end of the south range, there is a plainer arch-braced roof.

Bowhill is the only surviving example in Exeter of a fifteenth-century manor house.

Sources
Transactions Devonshire Association Devon
Cornwall Notes and Queries

About Ethel Lega Weekes and Arthur Everett

Anyone keen on the city's history can be grateful to Ethel Lega Weekes and Arthur W. Everett, who, with their work, have so interestingly contributed to the knowledge we have of Exeter's past. Sometimes they collaborated; her contributions concentrating on history, his being mostly about the archaeological or architectural aspect.

Ethel Lega Weekes, Fellow of the Royal Historical Society, who died in 1949 at the age of 85, was widely known for her antiquarian research work, and her contributions in Devon and Cornwall Notes and Queries and in the Transactions of the Devonshire Association make rewarding reading.

Among her works are 'Some Studies in the Topography of the Cathedral Close' (1915); 'History of Buckerell Bore' (1927); and in collaboration with Arthur Everett, 'St. Martin's House-on-the-Wall, Cathedral Close' (1935). Ethel Lega Weekes was so keen on accuracy that she would not publish anything which could not be proved as fact.

It was said that the most valuable of the causes she had furthered was the preservation of the remains of Polsloe Priory.

She had settled with her mother in Exeter at Varnello (the house is still there at No. 133 Topsham Road), and it is where she died, and where her mother had died in 1924. Part of her surname and the name of the house recall Ethel Lega Weekes's noble Italian ancestry on her mother's side: her maternal grandmother's father was Antonio del Zambelli della Lega di Varnello. Ethel's father, Ansel Weekes, was American and she spent part of her childhood and youth at Aramattapoisett, Mass. The East Devon Library (Westcountry Studies, Exeter) has recently acquired diaries of hers and two charming little pieces she wrote when she was four and five years old.

Arthur W. Everett, Fellow of the Society of Antiquaries and a member of the Vernacular Architecture Society, died at the age of 90 in 1979. He was self-taught in the subjects for which he became well known in Devon, and because of his high regard for accuracy in his observations and conclusions, his discerning judgement was much valued, and his help gratefully acknowledged by academics.

Buildings, above and below ground level, had fascinated him since his youth, and his knowledge was thorough. It included that of the ancient quarries from which came the stones used in the local buildings. He was also familiar with the plans of medieval monasteries, and with the different styles of ecclesiastical and domestic architecture.

He seems to have been in charge of most of the archaeological excavations carried out in Exeter between the two wars. His careful examination, surveys, measured drawings and descriptions of ancient structures were a befitting complement to their history which had been researched and written by Ethel Lega Weekes, as in the case of Bowhill, St Loyes Chapel, and St Katherine's Priory (Polsloe). He too was a contributor to *Devon and Cornwall Notes and Queries and the Transactions of the Devonshire Association*.

His work included the discovery below ground level, some 40 years ago, of a massive thirteenth-century wall which was probably the remains of St Thomas's Chapel (swept away by floods in the early-fifteenth century); the discovery of medieval tiles at St Katherine;s Priory, Polsloe, and the identification of their patterns and the finding there, of an ancient kiln where pottery was made from nearby clay. He also left interesting descriptions of fifteenth-century houses in Bear Street which were demolished in 1938. He made his own drawings and took his own photographs.

His work also took him outside Exeter, and his advice was sought on rebuilding and restoring.

Arthur Everett was born in Exeter and had lived for a considerable time in Old Tiverton Road when he died.

Arthur Everett and Miss Lega Weekes discussing one of Exeter's ancient buildings, c.1930.

CHAPTER 39

Barley Lane to Exwick Hill

There were still, until the 1960s, perhaps surprisingly, many 'country' walks which could be enjoyed by Exeter people if.first they took a city bus to its terminus. One of these delightful walks was from the top of Dunsford Hill along Barley Lane, and to Exwick (from which one can return to the city centre by walking across the river bridge and taking a bus at St David's Station).

Not so long ago, extensive views from peaceful green slopes, towards the city on one side, and towards the moor on the other, could delight the walker almost all along the route. Now, some of these hillsides are covered with the sores of poorly designed houses, while others have been churned into clods of mud in preparation for further ravage. It is disturbing that planning permission can be obtained for such density of unsuitable structures on such beautiful sites.

At the Dunsford Hill end of Barley Lane, there had been for some time a few bungalows opposite the grounds of Crossmead, but the view between the bungalows, and the sight of the grounds of this University hall of residence, were a good start for the walk. Now, in these grounds, has sprung up a screen of living-quarters formed by alternating strips of glass and brick. This is architecturally regrettable in any case, and would be on any site.

From the highest point of Croft Chase, one of the roads which spread like a huge spider-web to cover the whole flank of the hill that faces the city, Barley Lane used to narrow back into its original width. Here, a few minutes away from the bus stop, one was in the country. Now, this part of Barley Lane has been stretched into a new-estate width. On the right, incongruous in its mutated surroundings, the Georgian house Barley Croft – at some time known as Higher Barley or Little Barley – is still there, but its contemporary, Barley Farm, was swept away in the mid-1 960s.

Barley Lane takes its name from the Barley estate

The green hills of Exwick before major developments, c.1910.

was erected in the first half of the eighteenth century. It was altered to some extent in the early-nineteenth century and was probably stuccoed then.

The Sawles, Pinnock's indirect descendants, inherited the estate, but it was eventually divided between two members of the family. The Bowhill and Higher Barley part was sold in 1792. Barley House and the land round it, with carriage access through two drives (now Bowhay Lane and Isleworth Road), remained in the hands of the Sawle family until 1936. The County Council bought the house in 1938 for £1,250, and Barley House is now the Administrative Centre of Devon County Library Services.

Past Barley Croft, a new road has been made, and a visually deplorable crop of dwellings has been raised, but just beyond them, on the grass and among the trees, it is still the country. Here, unfortunately, the new road will continue and will be flanked by further eruptions of habitations whose spread along these hillsides, from the south-west to the north-west of the city, seems to be limitless. This is all the more regrettable when one remembers what a pleasure and a joy the sight of these lovely green hills was from the city itself.

But from the point where this new road of Nadder Park joins the widened Barley Lane, the old lane

which was once part of the Bowhill estate. This would have extended from Dunsford Hill to Redhills, and from Barley Lane to Buddle Lane. Bowhill, the fifteenth-century manor house, still stands (as we have seen in a previous chapter) on Dunsford Hill. It was John Pinnock (who had inherited the estate from his mother, the daughter of Thomas Carew, Recorder of Exeter in 1676), who built Barley House.

It is made of the local volcanic stone, which was quarried at various points near Barley Lane, and it

'The Hermitage', Exwick.

Houses being built on the Exwick Hills as seen from Peterborough Road.

View from Peterborough Road looking towards Exeter, 1980.

continues to the left unspoilt, up the hill and north-ward. Suddenly, it is all as it was: a very narrow road, trees, hills and ever changing views on both sides as we walk along towards the junction with the Old Okehampton Road and the few houses of Whitestone Cross.

Another lane from here leads to Exwick. Like Barley Lane, in the 1960s its course took one through a peaceful, hilly countryside, houses appearing only as one had almost reached Exwick, at the top of Exwick Hill.

The lane is still very much as it was, from Whitestone Cross to the grounds of Cleve House. But here, just before the narrow road turns sharply to the left, where, on the south side, green fields used to be, there is now a deep gash named Peterborough Road, along which is a sad display of wretchedly flat-faced dwellings of simulated stone.

Cleve, probably built in the late-seventeenth century, was bought for £3,000 in 1705 by Thomas Northmore from the Gubbs family. It remained the Northmore family seat for a considerable time, but it

View from Mount Dinham of Exwick, c.1940.

has now been used for many years as a centre where dogs are trained to guide the blind.

From Cleve, as we continue on our way to Exwick, because the lane is still intact for some 300 yards, the sudden appearance of a spread of unimaginativelyconceived new houses on both sides comes as a shock. The sprawl of Exwick Middle-School and its deplorable environment of characterless houses is an example of how not to build on such a site. Here and there, nostalgically, we can enjoy stretches of country hedges, left where no access was needed to one of the structures of the new development.

But where the lane picturesquely curved to the left between trees, it has been straightened, and what remains of the trees and of the banks in which they grew, is now enclosed behind railings. Further on, we come to a few much older houses, in front of which the original country lane hedge had been left intact. It still is so far.

Past these houses, we now have to cross a wide road. It is called Moorland Way where it climbs northward on our left. In a straight line with it, Knowle Drive is on our right and goes south, downhill, towards other new roads and Exwick Road. These new roads, whose houses are neither worse nor better than those of the various estates which

have sprung up between Dunsford Hill and Exwick Hill, should never have been permitted to climb up the hill to the levels allowed by the planning authority. Certainly Knowle Drive should have ended short of Exwick Hill. To have allowed it to continue its ascent into Moorland way across Exwick Hill, thus ruthlessly cutting what was once a pretty country lane about to enter a village, is unforgivable.

Just beyond this odious junction, oddly, the lane (Exwick Hill) is itself again. True, where there were green fields just above the back of the Hermitage cottages, new structures now dominate, but the rest of the 'Hill' is very much as it was many years ago.

The delightful thatch-roofed Hermitage, whose two wings, surprisingly, have a difference in age of about 200 years (the older one probably dating from the sixteenth century), had links with both grist and fulling mills, which once gave Exwick its importance. At this house died Samuel Banfill in 1843 at the age of 81. He was one of the partners who had established a woollen manufactory and fulling mills at Exwick in the eighteenth century. One of these industrial buildings has survived. It is at the bottom of Exwick Hill, across the main road, being used as a laundry.

Later in the last century, the Hermitage was also

The view in the early 1980s.

the home of John Ellacott who worked for the Mallets. When their flour mill was closed in 1958, there had been mills at Exwick for 900 years. The existence of a mill there is recorded in the Domesday Book, and later, it became the property of the Benedictine monks of Cowick Priory until the Dissolution. It was on this site that W.R. Mallet erected in 1886 the flour mill which closed 21 years ago. It is on the main road to Cowley, about 300 yards from the eighteenth-century factory building, and is now unoccupied.

Although there were fulling mills at Exwick in the seventeenth century, there does not appear to have been a grist mill there between the sixteenth century and Victorian time. By the mid-1860s there was no longer a cloth factory at the village.

On Exwick Hill itself, between the Hermitage and St Andrew's Road, little seems to have changed, although some picturesque cottages there, were demolished some 20 years ago. But the rash of unsightly dwellings, disquietingly, is being allowed to spread northward, and one fears that it will not be very long before all the peaceful, green hills, as far as Cowley, are covered with these sores and patches.

Sources
Article on Exwick (Jacqueline Warren, *Express & Echo*, 6 April 1961)
Article on Barley Estate (J.W., *Western Morning News*, 17 November 1961)
Article on Bowhill (J.W., *Western Morning News*, 28 May 1968)
Deeds relating to Northmore & Gubbs families (in private hands)

Cowick Barton before restorations. (J.W.)

Cowick Barton in 1979, after its conversion into a public house in 1964.

CHAPTER 40

Cowick Barton

Two houses in Exeter are commonly referred to as 'The Tudor House'. But the one which was moved from Frog Street to West Street preceded the Tudor period by some 85 years, and the other, in Tudor Street, dates from some 50 years after that period! We have, however, one fair-sized house truly belonging to Tudor times, it is Cowick Barton (now a public house) off Cowick Lane. Its E-shaped plan is typical of those days.

The central building is joined at each end by a wing forming a right-angle with it, and in its centre, the porch and its two storeys above form another, shorter wing, parallel to the two end ones. The three wings are gabled and the windows have one, two or three stone mullions giving the windows respectively two, three or four lights. The house is built of the local sandstone and volcanic stone but most of it is plastered over. The interior has been modified for its present function, but one can still see interesting features such as the original stone fireplaces and moulded ceiling beams in what was once the kitchen and the hall. The hall fireplace has an unusual crenellated cornice supported by engaged columns. Above it is the date 1657, but it is not known with certainty whose coat of arms the badge showing three stars represents. This was discovered behind paper and plaster, after years of neglect, when the house was being carefully restored towards the end of the last century.

'Barton', a word of Anglo-Saxon origin (literally, 'an enclosure of barley'), means a farm. Cowick Barton owes its name to a farm on this site which

The hall fireplace of Cowick Barton.

belonged to Cowick Priory.

St Andrew's or 'Cowick' Priory itself was situated between the river and Okehampton Street (Flowerpot Field). Leading from the priory to the farm, there was a path, part of which, mentioned in ancient documents, was a right of way across people's land known as the Monks' Walk. Before the extensive late-Victorian development of the area, it was still possible to follow this footpath from Okehampton Street through the site of St Thomas pleasure ground and across St Thomas churchyard to Cowick Barton.

Cowick Priory, founded in the late-twelfth century as a cell to Bec Abbey in Normandy, was suppressed as an Alien Priory by Henry V in 1414; its revenues were then given to Eton College, but transferred later to Tavistock Abbey. Cowick Priory suffered a series of misfortunes. Its buildings were on one occasion severely damaged by fire, but mostly being so close to the river, they were regularly subjected to floods.

At first the inhabitants of the district worshipped at the priory church, however from 1259, when a chapel dedicated to St Thomas the Martyr was erected at the St Thomas end of Exe Bridge, until 1410 when this chapel was swept away by floods, it was there that the local people worshipped.

But until 1412 when St Thomas Church was built on the present site, and its churchyard became available as a burial ground, none of the people in the area could be buried near their church because of the proximity of the river. This was also the case for the monks of Cowick Priory themselves and the clergy who served the chapel of St Thomas the Martyr at the west end of the bridge. It seems that the burial place for all was then on the higher land which belonged to the monks of St Andrew's Priory, next to their farm of Cowick Barton.

After the Dissolution of the Monasteries, the land of Cowick Priory, including Cowick Barton, fell into the hands of John Russell (Lord Lieutenant of Devon) to whom Tavistock Abbey had been granted. The present house was probably built by him and it is possible that it incorporates part of a previous building on the site and that some of the stones from the priory itself were used. This would account for two kinds of stone being found in the building.

Because of the arms of Edward VI as Prince of Wales (ostrich feather, badge and initial letters E.P.) found in a stained-glass window of the hall, it is likely and consistent with the style, that the house was erected some time between 1539 when Russell received the land, and 1547 when the Prince became King Edward VI. The stained glass was removed in about 1920.

The Russells (Earls of Bedford) owned Cowick Barton until 1640. It was then acquired by various other families until it became the property of the White Abbotts.

John White Abbott (1763–1851) a surgeon by profession, became famous as a water-colourist (several of his paintings are at the museum in Queen Street). His son, grandson, great-grandson and great-great-grandson all owned Cowick Barton. John White Abbott, the artist's grandson, who was married in 1883, had the house carefully restored.

It was in his time, when workmen were digging to lay a drain across a field from the house, that on 9 August 1887 a huge, carved, thirteenth-century stone coffin was discovered (it is at St Nicholas Priory). A man aged 90 stated in 1969 that he well remembered the incident when, as a boy of 8, he had asked the men who had just found the coffin whether there had been anything in it and they had told him there had been 'a shape' inside, which went to dust when they lifted the lid. There is a possibility that this was the remains of Sir Hugh Courtenay who died in 1291 and was buried on this site.

Soon after the discovery, an examination of the ground where the coffin was unearthed showed it must have been the site of the ancient chapel of St Michael, and this particular spot that of its sanctuary. Other, similar walled graves were discovered nearby, and one of them contained a chalice. It is probable that it was here that were buried the members of the monastic community of Cowick Priory, and the clergy who served the chapel of St Thomas the Martyr at Exe Bridge.

In the summer of 1963, workmen digging at a nearby building site, also once part of the grounds of Cowick Barton, uncovered human bones. This was undoubtedly the site where people in the area were buried until 1412, before St Thomas churchyard became available.

Early in 1964, close to the sixteenth-century house, which was then being converted into a public house, workmen digging trenches for drains discovered fragments of two vessels. This pottery, which probably dates from the fourteenth century, would have been used at the farm on the site, which belonged to Cowick Priory.

The monastic land at Cowick Barton had become that of the sixteenth-century house, and its grounds were still extensive earlier in this century, but even before the brewery acquired the property in 1963, the house had lost most of the land which once surrounded it. Much of what remained is now a tarmacked car park.

Sources

A. Jenkins (1806), *History and Description of the City of Exeter and its Environs*

Charles Worthy, (1892), *History of the Suburbs of Exeter*

White's Directories

Burke's *Landed Gentry*

Express & Echo reports of discoveries at Cowick Barton, 1963–64.

Devon & Cornwall Notes & Queries.

CHAPTER 41

Various Losses without and within the City Wall

Whipton Barton

Hill Lane, off the Pinhoe road, is dominated by ten storeys of piled up flats. Whipton Barton stood on this site. Fifty years ago, here was the country, but until the early-1960s, it was still ALMOST the country: Hill Lane had retained its original hedge and cottages, as well as its old farm. With the wrenching away of the Barton, and the erection in its place of this dwelling tower called Rennes House, what had been left of a rural aspect vanished for ever from the area.

The history of Whipton Barton goes back to Saxon days; it is mentioned in the Doomsday Book. At the end of the twelfth century, it was given as part of Whipton Manor by its owner, William de Tracey, to Polsloe Priory. He had been involved in the murder of Thomas à Becket, and it was said that his gift was made in atonement for his crime.

At the Dissolution, the Barton was acquired by John Petre. It was his grandson, William Petre, who, in 1611, was murdered by Edward Drew of Killerton, on their way back to their respective homes after a jolly day, and a riotous night, in the ale-houses of the city. William's horse alone returned to Whipton Barton! The farmhouse, which was demolished in the early-1960s, dated mostly from the seventeenth century. It was built of red sandstone, but two of its sides were plastered over. The gate was a most interesting feature. It had an unusual pattern carved in the wood, and the pillar on the left bore the arms of John Banks, owner of the Barton at the end of the seventeenth century. The other pillar showed the arms of the Crossing family into which John Banks had married. A large stone sphere surmounted each pillar. The Rew family owned Whipton Barton for a considerable time until the beginning of this century. It was scheduled as an ancient monument, but from the moment it was acquired by Exeter City Council it was doomed.

Old Heavitree House

Between Church Street (Heavitree), Kingsway, and Meadow Way, stood Old Heavitree House. It was demolished in the early 1960s, and since then small houses have filled the site.

The origin of Old Heavitree House was an Elizabethan cob cottage bought in 1834 with 12 acres of land around it (this included the site of the new streets) by Richard Ford, artist, writer, and an

Whipton Barton in its rural days.

The Gate of Whipton Barton. Rennes House is now on the site of the Old Barton. (J.W.)

The demolition of Whipton Barton, 1963.

Richard Ford's 'Old Heavitree House' before its demolition in the early 1960s.

Until 1962 Exchange Lane was between the premises of Webber & Sons and those shown on this photo as 'Miss Kernick Costumier'.

Nos. 74 and 76 East Wonford Hill, early-eighteenth-century, demolished 1966.   (J.W.)

authority on Spain. He built the house (incorporating the cottage), and laid the gardens, with considerable thought and care, over six years. Heavitree House, under its elaborate chimneys and slate roof, and with its decorated dripstones and small gables over its windows, became a magnificent building, standing in exquisite grounds. It was still in all its splendour when the Vaughan-Robinson family acquired it in 1899, and throughout the childhood and youth of their eight children. In the words of one of them, 20 years ago, 'Till we grew up, our world was Heavitree House.'

Richard Ford's house had been fitted with carved woodwork, some of it from abroad. A Jacobean fireplace had been acquired at a house in Rack Street,

and the carved wood over the doors had once belonged to an old inn in South Street. In the gardens, there were trellis-covered walls running down to different levels in deep steps, terraces and lawns, and an elegant tower. All this was laid out in the Moorish style of southern Spain, where Ford had lived for several years.

His Spanish notebooks were a rich source of information for his work *A Hand Book for Travellers in Spain*, which turned out to be a masterpiece of the kind. No doubt the sight of his beautiful garden also inspired his wiriting.

In the Second World War, and after it, Heavitree House was ill-used as workshops, and neglected. Eventually, its grounds were taken over by a new housing estate, even before the house was pulled down. It was a Grade II building on the list of buildings of architectural or historic interest devised by the Minsitry of Town and Country Planning in 1947.

A considerable length of the colourful sandstone wall, which once surrounded the grounds of Old Heavitree House, remains as a retaining wall on the east side of Meadow Way.

Houses in East Wonford Hill

Nos. 74 and 76 East Wonford Hill were a fine pair of four-storey houses with truncated gables and dormer windows. The modillion under their cornice, their thick corner stones, and their wide-framed windows, flush with the walls, showed they had been built in the early-eighteenth century. They were demolished in 1966. Grass now grows on their site, and nearby, blocks of flats have been erected. These two houses were listed as Grade II buildings.

Exchange Lane

The premises of John Webber (Sports) Ltd, at No. 51 High Street until 1962, were not in themselves architecturally remarkable, but their shop front and elevation were in harmony with their environment. What

Late-seventeenth-century doorway facing Exchange Lane. Demolished mid-1960s. (J.W.)

Early-eighteenth-century staircase (above and panelling of No. 21 Cathedral Yard. Removed in the mid-1960s before a new building was erected on this site. (J.W.)

has replaced this building since 1963 is as unsuitable to the site as it could possibly be. It dates from a period when the average architect was not concerned (when 'in-filling') with the character of the area for which he was designing, but was determined to build in the fashion of the day. At the time this structure was erected the 'glass-house design' was in vogue. It faces what used to be Goldsmith Street.

Apart from its Georgian façade, No. 21 Cathedral Yard had such good features, that as well as being scheduled as Grade II, it had an additional entry in the Ministry's list: 'Very fine 18th century staircase and panelling. ('Starred' grading on account of interior.)' Every other baluster of the staircase was 'twisted', and alternate ones were, like the newel posts, 'fluted'. The step-ends had curved and scrolled mouldings, and the wood panelling on the wall followed a curve similar to that of the hand-rail along the two flights of shallow steps, which were turned in opposite directions by a small landing. These latter features, the panelling of the passage leading to the staircase, the round-headed window with the garland ornament below it, on the landing, were all typical of the late-seventeenth century or the early-eighteenth. So was an entrance door facing a courtyard called 'Little Exchange'. This doorway had a hood supported by consoles representing acanthus leaves, and its original door had 10 small panels. This interior of No. 21 Cathedral Yard was not only very fine, but unique in Exeter.

Permission to remove it and to demolish the house was granted to the Prudential Assurance Co. by the local authority and the Ministry of Housing and Local Government. A new building, with an imitation Georgian façade, has been erected on the site since 1965.

Until 1962, when the Webber premises were demolished, there had been a passageway from High Street to the Cathedral Yard, which was picturesque, full of interest, and convenient too. One entered it through a doorway adjoining the east side of No. 51 High Street, and one emerged from it through the doorway of No. 21 Cathedral Yard. From High Street or from Cathedral Yard, one went through a narrow covered passage first, before reaching the long, flagstoned, open court which was between them. Here, all round, hipped slate roofs with attractive, uneven lines, and windows flush with walls, showed the houses to be contemporary with No. 21 Cathedral Yard.

This short-cut from High Street to the Cathedral was called Little Exchange in the mid-eighteenth century, and later referred to as Exchange Lane. In the summer of 1962, its flagstones were ripped off, and its ground was dug at some depth for foundations, but at least, one sixteenth-century jug was found underneath!

The losses incurred by Exeter, considered so far in this chapter, were in each case due to the conscious determination by those involved to remove an

Conclusion

As we have seen in these chapters, Exeter has suffered much from the demolition of its buildings: some officially listed as of 'architectural or historic interest' (and given a high grading); others, less important in themselves, but forming a valuable contribution to the townscape of the city.

We have also seen that the original street pattern, which had been left practically unchanged for hundreds of years, or at least, which had remained easily traceable – and this was of immense interest to historians – has, since the last war, been lamentably disturbed and become, in some parts of the city, unrecognisable. This determination to bulldoze, widen and straighten streets, is not only the result of an insensitive conception for a city like Exeter, but it has also been found, more recently, to be an impractical notion. It is ironical that the local authority, having brutally widened the part of High Street which was badly damaged during the war, should have altered it again into a narrow channel for buses to slide through (across a pedestrian area!)

Apart from the war years, the most relentless destruction, that is, affecting the greatest number of buildings, occurred in the early 1960s. The demolition has, however, continued since, and is currently affecting a vast area (surrounded by Queen Street, High Street and Goldsmith Street) which looks as if it had been war-devastated. All the buildings which stood on these acres were perfectly sound.

As for the replacements which have been allowed to rise on the vacated sites, they are in most cases unsuitable for their environment. Architectural designs which are conceived in what is called the Spirit of the Age, reflect – and then inspire – the social idiosyncrasies of the time. It is unfortunate for cities like Exeter that the designs of architects who have built, sometimes successfully, on a large scale, on entirely new sites, in the Spirit of the Age, should appear in architectural publications. This is because these schemes provoke compulsive imitation (however smaller the scale has to be) from members of the profession who have not been endowed with enough aesthetic sensitivity, originality of mind and self-confidence, to avoid following what has become, or is about to become, the fashion, regardless of any other consideration.

Even when a mistake was made, in the past, regarding the suitability of a new building to a particular site in a city or town, at least the ill-effect was not on a large scale, simply because firms – mostly local or regional – and the premises they required in those days, were of a modest size.

But, for example, such buildings as the one occupied by Debenham's, at the junction of Sidwell Street with Longbrook Street, and the C&A structure, at the corner High Street–Queen Street, are distressing to look at, not only because their shapes, and some of

the materials and colour schemes used in them, do not fit in with their surroundings, but also because there is so much of them in width and length; and in the case of Debenham's, in height as well.

Fortunately, there seems to be emerging a new fashion which might be the result of protests over the years, from people outside the profession, who could not see why architects had to plant identical or similar structures anywhere in the world irrespective of the locality, its traditions and setting. For the last two years or so, not only have interesting façades been retained, on occasion, in shopping centres, but new buildings have stopped being squared off at the top, and dwelling-houses are no longer flat-faced and being erected in straight lines. The houses being built at the moment (1979) in Melbourne Place and Northernhay Street, for instance, are set at attractive angles; their lines form becoming recesses and protrusions; and their roofs (some with the added charm of dormer windows) are traditionally visible, and so are a pleasing feature in a city like Exeter.

But the first new scheme to be really successful in Exeter was the Shilhay housing estate. As we have seen in the chapter on the Exe Bridges, this thoughtfully conceived, attractive estate has been established on land which was once a centre of activity for Exeter's woollen trade.

As has been shown in this book, Exeter has lost far too many of its attractive features, and we, the authors, as we look at the city today and consider what has been done to it, can only console ourselves with the thought, 'it could have been even worse!'. Sadly, we see that only the Cathedral Close, the part of High Street which is near the Guildhall, and the stretch of Queen Street between Little Queen Street and Paul Street, are central areas of the city that have (mostly) been spared from wartime destruction, post-war demolition, and unsuitable reconstruction.

We much regret the razing to the ground of the vast area between Queen Street and Goldsmith Street, particularly since, in 1976, the local authority, before giving planning permission for the redevelopment of the site, had insisted that the character of what remained of the older part of Exeter in this area should be kept. The firm concerned had even stated that it was prepared to retain the façades of the buildings facing the Waterbeer Street pedestrian square!

Now we can only hope that the new scheme will be good, and admirably suited to its environment. We hope, too, past mistakes having been recognised, that in future wrong planning decisions will be avoided, and that what is worthy of preservation will be properly maintained and suitably incorporated into what may have to be rebuilt.

Exeter August 1979
J.W.